KYRIAKOS CHARALAMBIDES
Famagusta Regina

KYRIAKOS CHARALAMBIDES

Famagusta Regina

TRANSLATED BY
JOHN MILIDES

Arcadia

© Kyriakos Charalambides
Original publication in Greek:
Kyriakos Charalambides, *Ammochostos Vasilevousa*, Ermis, Athens, 1982
© John Milides, English translation

First published 2018 by ARCADIA
the general books imprint of
Australian Scholarly Publishing Pty Ltd
7 Lt Lothian St Nth, North Melbourne, Vic 3051
Tel: 03 9329 6963 / Fax: 03 9329 5452
enquiry@scholarly.info / www.scholarly.info

ISBN 978-1-925801-29-3

ALL RIGHTS RESERVED

Cover: Mosaic, Roman Baths of the Gymnasium at Salamis, Famagusta, Cyprus, 3rd century AD (Credit: Press and Information Office).

The publication of this translation was assisted by the Ministry of Education and Culture, Republic of Cyprus.

CONTENTS

Acknowledgements vii
Prologue by the poet viii
Introduction by Dr Thanasis Spilias xi

The beginning of a love affair   1
Imitation of defeat   4
The name of city   6
The rubbish truck   8
I saw her   10
Birth date of a horse   12
Lesson in archaeology   15
Cauldron   18
Birds   20
Colts and horses   22
To almighty God   25
Beginning of the Indiction   29
Good Friday   30
The perfect carbon   33
For the city that remained faithful to her comrades   36
Headless statue   38
The hull of a ship   40
The element of water   42
The voice of blood   46
A magical game   48
Towards Trachea   50
Submission   52

The angry sun 54
The third dimension 56
The rise from sleep 58
Endeavour 61
The trunk trembles 63
By affinity 65
Abolition of the moon 67
Body of clay 69
The difference 71
After midnight 73
Seizure of a city 75
Madonna of the Golden Cave 77
Resurrection hymn 80
Effigy 82
For the city which voted for those who brought her to this point 84
The strange dream 86
March towards Famagusta 90
The story of the civil guard 93
Ardana 96
Winged sun 99
The wind god 100
The waves 102
Tympani of love 104
Baton 106
Free-field style vase 114

About the author and the translator 123

ACKNOWLEDGEMENTS

I wish to thank the following people for supporting the publication of this translation.

Dr Thanasis Spilias, for his deep knowledge of the Greek language and the Cypriot dialect; for providing insight and advice on the language of the original work and for writing the introduction.

Mrs Marian Spilias, English teacher par excellence, for proofreading and meticulous editing.

Ms Theano Iliades, for word-processing and final proofreading.

Dr Tom Petsinis, for encouragement and support.

The Ministry of Education and Culture, Republic of Cyprus.

The poet, Kyriakos Charalambides, for his poetry that dares to confront the human condition and create new poetic pathways to explore the soul in its moments of suffering and redemption.

John Milides

PROLOGUE BY THE POET

At times, art plays the same ritual role as the people who are gathered around the altar of a tragedy that has struck their own country. It also plays the role of transforming sorrow into a song, transforming lamentation into a hymn. The meaning of this, is crystal clear: that we can determine, via the name Famagusta, the visualisation of the symbols of our diffused worship, the embracing of the vision, the passionate portrayal and simultaneously, the mythical narration of the hardships of our long-suffering people. Hence, the secret relationship between art and life is revealed.

The poet Laureate George Seferis said that when he visited Cyprus in 1954, Cyprus had broadened his view of the Hellenic world. Similarly, I want to believe that my poems in *Famagusta Regina*, broaden the vision of a city, which in this case symbolises the whole of Cyprus and transcends the land. It symbolises mankind in its ecumenical dimension.

I am often asked what the title *Famagusta Regina* means, as it has unexpectedly become an intellectual logo of the city.

Firstly, Famagusta, like Alexander the Great, "still lives, still reigns and conquers the world", as folklore has it. Famagusta has transcended its territory: the invaders have turned it into a ghost-town; the poet has turned it into a town of vision, a town possessing the strength to resist its tragedy. But tragedy cannot exist without its "hubris" and the final "catharsis."

This poetical work begins with the turning of the head up-side-down looking at "the sky with its stars bloodied." It is the time of sunset, the time when "blood" floods the sky, until, through choruses, rituals, self-realisation and exodus, we arrive at catharsis. The work finishes with the verse "the stars of the sky have been purified."

I won't describe the work; I will only highlight some symbols:

Famagusta suffered the fate of conquered cities, the same way Constantinople (the Queen of Cities) was conquered by the same Turkish conqueror.

Famagusta reigns (dominates over our hearts); she is the queen in the sky of our heart; an object of a sacred love.

Famagusta reigns (like the sun that heads west and reddens the sky) with the absolute certainty that it will rise the next day.

Famagusta is elevated from an earthly to an interstellar level. It discards its mortal face and gleams in the light of the Kingdom of the Skies. No sacrilegious hand can touch her any longer.

Famagusta verifies in analogy the epigram by the Cypriot poet Vasilis Michaelides regarding the national martyr Archbishop Kyprianos (publicly hanged by the Ottomans in Nicosia on 9 July 1821): "You, who died for enlightenment / rise to see the sun; / wake to see that your blood/ has turned into a kingdom."

There comes a time when objects themselves become transubstantiated through the gaze of the eye. They obtain a dimension of entrancement; they become what we may call "a torchbearer's ascent", reminding us of the prophet Elias who ascended the skies in a chariot of fire – we commemorate him on 20 July, the same date as the Turkish invasion of Cyprus. In other words, the prophet prefigured Jesus on His way to Emmaus, when His disciples walked with Him, conversed with Him and did not recognise Him. Luke, the evangelist, describes the scene adding: "Then their eyes opened and they recognised Him; and He vanished from their sight." The inference is clear: We can see clearer, only when we lose the precious possession we owned. We behold it then, in its esoteric dimension, at a level of indestructibility and awe; the predetermined Kingdom of Heaven.

Through these images, I propose to delineate the framework within which to view the Cypriot tragedy. Our people will endure mentally when they discern the secret meaning of the cycle of their suffering; if they would transfuse the blood of the torchbearer's ascent to the image of the ghost-town; if they can conquer their heartbreak with a more ecumenical notion of the world and of history.

To grasp these things, we need to reclaim such a city. It is up to us to decide how near or how far this city is, and how distant we are from it. It depends on us and on the quality of our pain; a pain that is transformed into true bliss due to the magical sorrow which has its own power: to remain inconsolable.

Kyriakos Charalambides

INTRODUCTION

Dr Thanasis Spilias

Lecturer in Ancient Greek, La Trobe University
Senior Lecturer in Greek Studies, Deakin University

The city of Famagusta has correctly been described as a "ghost city".[1] Since 1974, it has been uninhabited – "with no bread, no water, no news." It remains an open wound for Greek Cypriots since they can only mourn its condition as they gaze at it from afar – "To look at you four miles away / and to imprint your image in my mind". The rightful inhabitants have been deprived even of the freedom to visit it. The Turks on the other hand, use the city as a negotiating or bargaining chip at endless discussions regarding a solution for the issues resulting from the invasion of Cyprus.

The Turkish invasion of the island in July 1974 had a huge impact on the island and on the lives of Greek Cypriots. Because of that invasion, the island was divided into two with the Turks taking possession of the northern part while the Greeks – being 80% of the island's population at the time – were left with the southern section only. Consequently, the large majority of Greek Cypriots from the northern part had to forcibly abandon their homes and possessions and move – as refugees – to the free southern part of Cyprus. Sadly, a significant number of Cypriot soldiers, as well as civilians, remain unaccounted for to this day.

---

1   Kechagioglou, 1983, p. 75.

It was not the first time that Cyprus had become a target for invaders. The island had fallen into the hands of foreign occupiers on many occasions in the past mainly due to the fact that Cyprus constitutes a cross-road at the junction of three continents – Asia, Africa and Europe. From antiquity, owing to its unique geographical location, the island has been the "apple of discord" as it was always coveted by the neighbouring countries, some of which, at different times, not only conquered and inhabited it, but left behind elements of their cultural heritage when they were finally ousted.

The ancient Greek civilization of Cyprus is evident in the wealth of archaeological excavations and findings and numerous historical and mythological references which abound in Ancient Greek literature and culture. However, the invaders who had conquered the island clearly left their own stamp on it, and to a certain degree, they influenced the island's image and its culture, and this is evident in many of the poems in this collection.

Readers of the poems in *Famagusta Regina* need to bear this background in mind, as it sheds light on the meaning of the poems and gives a deeper insight into many aspects alluded to in them.

Mention has been made above of how the Turkish invasion of 1974 drastically changed the fate of the island and that of its inhabitants. As the poet himself puts it, quoting Vitsentzos Kornaros (an acclaimed poet of Renaissance Crete) "the nature of things has been reborn anew".[2] And this new state of affairs, as might have been expected, revived and re-invigorated the literary output of Cyprus, feeding it thematically with material that resonates with the recent historical reality. Cypriot writers, folk poets and literary poets now draw anew upon their most recent excruciating and still raw experiences, and as a result many of them have produced literary works of deep passion and high quality.

Among such works, the present collection proudly holds a distinguished place. It was written between 1979 and 1981 and was

---

[2] Vitsentzos Kornaros, *Erotokritos,* trans. Gavin Betts, Stathis Gauntlett and Thanasis Spilias, Byzantina Australiensia 14, Melbourne, 2004, p. 106 (C 1277).

published in 1982. By that time, the poet had already produced examples of writing that had given a clear indication of literary worth. However, this new publication arguably constitutes the pinnacle of Cypriot literature. It has been lauded by prominent scholars and critics and after its publication, the poet was awarded prestigious literary prizes. Moreover, it has been proposed that Charalambides should be given a place among the most prominent of contemporary Greek poets.

As has been stated above, the poet draws upon, and is directly influenced by, the tragic events in Cyprus and the new historical reality that became the norm after the Turkish invasion of 1974. The reader will obviously realise – and this has been pointed out by both critics and the poet himself – that the poems do not cover only the brief time-span from 1974 onwards; they also encompass the lengthy history of Cyprus from prehistoric times to more recent years. Through the poems, the reader will not only glean a clear picture of Greek antiquity, which is apparent everywhere on the island, but will also be ushered into the Byzantine era and the time of the Venetian rule, as well as the Greek and western traditions that flourished in Cyprus. Throughout this lengthy course, and despite the sporadic foreign influences, the island's "diachronic" Greekness has remained steadfast. The poems in this collection reveal that even in the sensitive sphere of religion, many pagan elements have survived to the present day. For example, "the sacred cow-eyed wife of Zeus" lends some of her characteristics to the Virgin Mary cradling the baby Jesus – as happens in the poem *Madonna of the Golden Cave* where "The cow-eyed and humble Virgin / holds her Son in her arms in by-gone times".

The title of the collection – *Famagusta Regina* or *Ammochostos Vasilevousa* as in the original – with its various connotations, has preoccupied and perplexed the critics. This is partly because the participle "Vasilevousa" (which determines or describes the preceding noun – that is, the city of Famagusta) functions as a polysemic word and therefore lends itself to different interpretations and explanations.

Traditionally, the royal title "Vasilevousa" was used to refer exclusively to Constantinople, the "Queen of Cities", which for centuries constituted the cultural, spiritual and religious centre of Europe and in particular, of the Middle East. Ultimately, "Constantinople Vasilevousa" – "the city that Reigns" – would fall to the Turkish invaders, as would the City of Famagusta some centuries later. On a different note, the verb "vasilevo" (to set) – as in the setting of the sun – alludes to the end of the city of Famagusta which has "set" (died) and has ascended to the kingdom of heaven. Notably, in Greek, the term "kingdom" (of heaven) (Vasileia) and the word "reigning" (vasilevousa) are derived from the same root and sound similar. The setting of the sun, therefore, presupposes a new dawn or is followed by the sun's rising again.

Be what it may, Famagusta reigns in the heart of the poet. It is the dearly beloved city with its historical, cultural and spiritual connotations that he mourns and yearns for, but it is also the city he proudly celebrates throughout the collection.

This collection consists of 47 poems in total, which are set out in chronological order from the summer of 1979 until the autumn of 1981. According to the poet, the chronological sequence of the poems and every detail in the collection have been thoroughly considered and well-studied, "as happens with a wall painting," as he explains. We must bear this in mind as Charalambides confesses to having studied *visual arts and cinematography* and he transfers aspects of the techniques of these fields to his writing. *"I paint with words,"* he points out characteristically. "The words in my poems are substitutes for the shapes and the colours of the images". Such prowess embellishes and enriches the imagery in his poems and enhances the narrative which is "optically" and "orally" presented in a balanced interchange of "show and tell".

According to the poet, from a thematic viewpoint, *Famagusta Regina* "constitutes a point of reference for the Cypriot tragedy as a whole." As G. Kechagioglou succinctly puts it: "From different points of view, all the poems serve as a "portrayal" or "reconstruction" of Famagusta within its diachrony and synchrony [...] not only of the city (and by extension of Cyprus) [...] but also from moments of the personal history and the internal adventures of the poet."[3]

As is well known, the "synchronic" aspect covers the events from the day of the Turkish invasion up to the end of the writing of the poems (1981). On the other hand, the "diachronic" aspect covers the historical and political events on the island in totality. Vivid indeed is the portrayal not only of Famagusta but of the whole island and that of the poet's experiences as well. Naturally, the poet grieves for the afflictions that have been imposed upon his homeland, yet even from within these tragic events, it is possible to derive some hope. "Suffering" can beget "knowledge" the poet would say, meaning that we can learn even from our mistakes; we can come to realise things about ourselves and our history and gain knowledge from, or be taught something by these.

The word "tragedy" which is mentioned above could perhaps be used to describe the work as a whole in the sense that the progression of the poems acts as a "theatrical" tragedy. For example, after the poems enumerating the afflictions suffered by the city collectively, ("You are surrounded by barbed wire now") after achingly outlining the upheaval of the refugees and the island's dismemberment, ("Half the city in Larnaca and the rest in Limassol / with some remnants in Nicosia and Paphos, / making up the city I loved") after mourning the slaughter of innocents and those unaccounted for, ("One day in her mass grave you found / the hand of a child, and on another day, its head") after lamenting the plunder of priceless archaeological treasures, ("The limbs of ancient colossi are scattered; / I fear, we must look for them / in foreign galleries ...") at the end of the collection, "catharsis" prevails as it does in an ancient Greek tragedy: The "bloodied stars" of heaven in the first poem will again make their appearance in the last verse of the poem with which the collection ends. However, here, the stars have been cleansed; "The stars of the Heavens have been purified."

---

3   Kechagioglou, 1983, p. 77.

The same idea of purification or catharsis also appears in the poem *Good Friday*. Here the poet alludes to the ritual closure of ancient Greek tragedy where a sacrifice brings about catharsis in the end:

> *What ram, or other sacrificial offering now sprouts in place of Isaak,*
> *Iphigenia and other martyrs of the theatre?*

However, the cathartic stanzas on which the poem concludes is uplifting:

> *You are surrounded by graces,*
> *flyers of the resurrection and erotic guitars.*

Famagusta Regina has been described as a difficult set of poems and one that is hard to access. The collection is seen as a work which, in order to be understood, needs to be looked at and studied holistically, as a complete creation, divided into different parts. One aspect that adds to its difficulty, but which both broadens and deepens the work endowing it with a further dimension, is the intertextuality that characterises it. This intertextuality holds the key to unlocking the poems' many obscurities. As the reader will discover, the poet often "communicates" with other fellow artists; he converses creatively with them, incorporating quotations from, and allusions to, their works; he extends some of their ideas, he objects, he criticises, and he judges.

Furthermore, in this collection there is frequent and constructive interchange of ideas between the poet and major Greek poets – Cavafy, Seferis, Solomos and so on – as well as between the poet and other renowned literary figures like Dante, Shakespeare etc. The many such references, which surely might hamper the lay reader, may possibly pose difficulties for the informed reader as well. In both cases, the poet's notes – with explanations and comments – direct the reader to sources that greatly assist him/her in coming to grips with such inaccessible, but important references.

On a similar note, the poet's knowledge of antiquity and of ancient Greek literature in all its phases, as well as his thorough acquaintance with Cypriot history and culture are as important as intertextuality. Elements of these two fields abound throughout the collection. Here again, the poet refers to well-known literary works reconstructing and incorporating many of their elements into visions of his own. In as far as archaeological topics are concerned, apart from the numerous references to archaeological treasures throughout the collection, in the poem *Lesson in Archaeology* the reader is offered evidence of the poet's interest in, and personal experiences of, this topic. With regards to the history of Cyprus, a good overview would be gained through a study of the poem *Baton* which spans the island's history from prehistoric times to the present.

However, the narration of the island's history is not confined to the mere cataloguing of events. Indeed, the past functions as a correlation with the present. This means that although the poet alludes to people and events from ancient history, he is clearly referring to people and events in the present:

> *The message that the city had been conquered*
> *for the umpteenth time was brought by a Turk*
> *after he got it from a Greek traitor,*
> *who got it from an Englishman, and the Englishman*
> *from a Turk, and he, from a Venetian, a Frank and a Templar.*

This correlation is made even more evident in the "explanation" inserted at the end of the poem *Birth date of a horse*

> *My own note: When we say Trojans*
> *We don't mean those much-afflicted people,*
> *or Hecuba and Priam and Hector.*
> *Those Trojans entered with us*
> *among the horses of Engomi, with their god Apollo.*

Here again, the numerous explanations and comments, either within the collection or in the poet's notes at the end of it, constitute an invaluable guide for the full understanding and interpretation of the work.

Worthy of note is also the collection's multi-faceted narration. That is, the co-existence of different types of narrative – poetry (which naturally constitutes the bulk of the text), storytelling and theatre which of course are presented poetically. As for the poet/narrator, he exploits poetic liberties to transform himself into a lover, an orator, a wanderer etc., depending on what best serves the narrative. Indeed, in one of the more memorable poems, *Free-field Style Vase*, the poet, now transformed into a "bird-visitor," – as M. Pieris[4] would have it – presents the story through the unusual viewpoint of a bird. This is not only because this is now the only way for anyone to "visit" the imprisoned city of Famagusta, but also because the bird persona is very commonly used in Greek folk poetry and hence, draws upon the heart strings of any Greek reader who would be familiar with the many such poems alluded to here. For instance, the verse "My ring fell in the lake of Saint Luke" is an allusion to the well-known and much loved demotic song "Arta's Bridge" which centres on the tragic figure of the Master Builder's wife who was tricked into being sacrificed for an ulterior motive (to make the bridge hold firm).

In conclusion, it must be noted that *Famagusta Regina* contains many autobiographical elements. "The whole book is me!" the poet says, "Me and the testimony of my soul, the memories, the feelings, the reactions and the self-reflections".[5] Thus, this collection exudes the unique relationship that the poet has with his beloved city, which he wanted to immortalise through his poetry. The result is truly admirable. The collection has received accolades from scholars and has been described as "The most accomplished book of poetry of 1982"[6] while

---

4   Pieris, 1991, p. 288.
5   Charalambides, vol. 2, p. 294.
6   Kechagioglou, 1983, p. 78.

M. Pieris claims it is "equivalent to the best poetic works of (Greek) contemporary poetic production."[7]

BIBLIOGRAPHY

Vitsentzos Kornaros, *Erotokritos,* trans. Gavin Betts, Stathis Gauntlett and Thanasis Spilias, Byzantina Australiensia 14, Melbourne, 2004

In the Greek language

Charalambides, K., Slippery Post, vol. 1 & 2, Agras, Athens, 2009

Herodotou, M., "The cornerstone of the soul" – An introduction to the collection Famagusta Regina, *Antipodes* 25–26, Melbourne, 1994

Kechagioglou, G., "From the enclaved ghost-city to the eminent City of the Ascension," *Diavazo 62,* Athens, 1983

Pieris, M., *From the share of Cyprus,* Kastaniotis, Athens, 1991

Tsianikas, M., *The name of Famagusta,* Indictos, Athens, 2003

---

7   Pieris, 1991, p. 286.

Then their eyes opened and they recognized Him; and He vanished from their sight.

Luke, 24:31

THE BEGINNING
OF A LOVE AFFAIR

I had turned my head upside-down gazing
at the sky and its bloodied stars.
Your sculpted stone touched
your Holy Belt[8] and your slipshod eyes
gave pulse to my unruly breath.
Prickly pears mark where the eternal city began.

Now that I am near you, city surrounded by iron,
I should return some things I borrowed
from you forty years ago.

City! With the moon's crescent in your hair,
the bareheaded sun,
the fragrance dressed
in the plumes of May,
the sea, like the leaf of a maple tree.

I miss you, I long for you …
You, who once were a spotless petticoat,
and later, at the murdered President's junction,[9]
an immovable corpse, a raided sea.

---

8   Holy Belt: The Church of the Holy Belt of Mary in Famagusta was renovated in 1951. The students of the Primary School opposite the church had interesting experiences; the poet was an eleven-year-old student at the school.

9   the murdered President's junction: President Kennedy Avenue, Famagusta, along the coastline of the city.

As the daylight leans to my side,
you become mine for ever – but what's the use?
You are now surrounded by barbed wire.[10]
A whole city imprisoned.
Destined to remain trapped, motionless.
With no bread, no water, no news.
On a terrace, the baby's clothes
are washed by the rain and ironed by the wind.

Listen to me now, because I shall speak no more:
In a few years you will be returned
to the ownership of everyone –
the legal owners of the land-lots, the houses,
the orchards, the windmills and the sea,
the central square, the marketplace.
The whole Municipality with its band and the Public Garden,
will be given back to you, again.
And, pleased with the new undertakings,
you will leave your forgotten love to destiny.

City of my former footsteps, your pinnacle does not reach
the sphere of my gaze.
I move further but there is no sky.
I embrace the stars; they shine brilliantly.
I grab a pitch fork and I winnow
the hay of my life over empty cities.
The world is a profitable profession.
My destiny, of course, is to fail.

Eyeball white everywhere.
A day that's forty yards long,
Now surrounds your enemy ... myself.

---

10   barbed wire: Famagusta is a city occupied by the Turkish Army since 14 August 1974; the year of the Turkish invasion of Cyprus.

I know you are wasting away in your ordeal;
a city, yet you are becoming an illusion …
No eyes watch over you, no human hands dig your soil,
no roses and unruly children nurture you.

Many people full of hope and somewhat optimistic,
say: "When we return, you are welcome to visit us."
Even the day-before-yesterday, an old-man – a refugee – said to me:
"I am not going back to my bad old neighbourhood,
there are louts there and noise.
When we return to Famagusta,
I have arranged to move to another dwelling;
it belonged to a gentleman who passed away."

So many deaths; so much hope of a return!
The two of us, I can see, have unfinished business yet.

June 1979

IMITATION OF DEFEAT

I shut windows and doors
so that the city will not be dispersed into the yard.
And I collect her from under the bed,
from the closet, from behind the picture frames,
the steam cooker, the fly-leaves of books.

Oh, the books![11] It's because of them that
there is decency and beauty in the world …
Those who disagree, can leave. Beware of the snow!

And now, the few of us friends who have remained
can speak without curtailments.
Remember my words about the books …
When the city entered the antechamber
of the vastness of doom,
we locked the dog and the rooster
in the living room, and we ran off to the fields.

Eating bitter almonds and locusts,
we came into contact with our native land,
when we were shown heads of snakes
with their frightful tongues pointing at us.

You will have realised that other things come to mind

---

11 the books: cf. Anton Chekhov, *The Cherry Orchard*, Act 1: "My dear and honoured case! I congratulate you on your existence, which has already for more than a hundred years been directed towards the bright ideals of good and justice."

as I struggle to fathom the city;
darkness encroaches against my will.
For I can't forget; I long for the city.
It is her, and only her, that I want to mark out.

But I can't. I am unable, even though I take
well-founded dynamite,
rugs and trays and quilts,
plants, mirrors, plates and forks,
buckets, the fridge and the television.

I do not know if I am convincing; it seems the city
does not trust me of late.
I shall therefore open a book
to find conspiracies, powerful plots,
magical theories and analgesics.

Like the old philosopher[12] I shall declare: "Nothing exists!
I have laid down my weapons at an auction
without pettiness and mysticism."

Thus, spoke the old poet,
taking out his key of silence.

February 1980

---

12 the old philosopher: Refer also to Paliosofos (meaning old philosopher) a village in the Kyrenia district of Cyprus, now under Turkish occupation. It took its name from the Greek scholar-philosopher George Lapithis, a close friend of King Hugh IV (1324–1359 AD).

THE NAME OF A CITY

Now happiest, loveliest in yon lovely Earth,
Whence sprang the "Idea of Beauty" into birth.
                                            Edgar Allan Poe

Could "Famagusta", the name of a city, be fake?
A contrived separation of space and land of utopia?
Time made of finely crafted sand
as you gaze at her white breasts?[13]

Who would disagree?
    – You forgot the refugees who are
standing opposite her,[14] waving to her.
They know how to weep, how to break their hearts
with sea-shells. Their car and tractor engines
are started up ready to go,
facing towards the guard-posts of the Turks
the tanks of the enemy.

How could you speak like that – I wouldn't believe it of you! –
about those who are like friends and brothers.

You misunderstood me, hypocritical reader.
Perhaps I only see Famagusta which I love.

---

13   white breasts: before the building frenzy with which Famagusta lost its original character, the city was surrounded by beautiful white sand hills close to the sea.

14   standing opposite her: from the village of Deryneia, Famagusta is situated at an arm's length. The Turkish army guarding posts are facing the refugee settlements.

We shall live together – Death and Life.
I know it, I believe it, I will even sign it.
For there is no death, no enemy, no deception;
that is why I called the city fake,
the city where I was born forty centuries ago.

But when I look through the binoculars
at the imperceptible crack between her breasts,
when, from her intoxicating breath,
I judge how many boats have sunk or ran aground,
and I see people around me exclaiming
"There's my house." What can I do then?
I grieve dearly,
I use a word spiked with nails,
I shout out "enemy" increasing the sorrow
of utopia – your words pierce my soul
my tyrant of love, my Master, a playing card.

An incarnate creation gleams around your hair.
We offer water, sweets, a gentle touch.
But what do you give us in return? Eh? We are asking for a city,
if it is the one where we spent our best years
or the one we abandoned to the four winds.

August 1980

THE RUBBISH TRUCK

Then the rubbish truck came
and collected the whole city.
While the truck-forks were turning her to pulp
I heard heart-rending cries: "Aquarius, help!"

"What is it?" I wondered. It seems that a city is being crushed!
I leave the walnuts I was halfway through cracking
and I run to protect the windows, the doors,
the belltowers, the kitchenware, the sofas and garden beds.

I get into the truck too, to stop the death and the rain
like the poor Negroes[15] in Miami.
In vain did Martin, the son of Luther, from a generation of kings,
called out to me: "Orthodox Aquarius, watch out!"
I ignored him; I stuck to my tune and I was caught out.
I had a hand, a leg and an ear,
both eyes and both lips cut off – I became an artery
through which the broken glass and nails of the city
flowed by.

In my sleep of course – I forgot to say,
all these images belong in a dream with a happy conclusion –
a *"happy end"*.

---

15 Negroes of Miami: in 1968, on a rainy night, two black men in Miami hid inside a rubbish truck. Two white men started up the truck and crushed them to death. Around the same time, Martin Luther King went to Memphis to lead a protest march; he was murdered there (4 April 1968).

But, what will always remain in my mind –
(the only thing not lost, nor sleeping)
is the city which I managed to feel
at a twist of the truck's fork;
she lay on my chest
like a little domestic cat, a loyal dog.
Telling me fairy tales; incredible things!
The two of us would pass, she says, through the arches
that birds form in the sky.
And from the hook where they hang an egg,[16]
we'll go and fetch water.
You, flying with heaps of wings
and I, very close to you, like a seagull.

I forced a grin
knowing for a long time how powerful
my city's physique has been.
I hold her in my hand,
she, a partridge and I, a dove –
how do birds and their names
relate to all this, since
foreign armies tear out their guts.

August 1980

---

16   the hook where they hang an egg: a symbolic custom on the last Sunday of the Halloween. After dinner, all family members try to "catch" with their mouth open a boiled egg tied to a hook hanging from a stick. The symbolism has to do with Lent. Catching the egg closes the mouth for fasting; the cracking of eggs on the night of the Resurrection, restores life to normality.

I SAW HER

It was my city that I saw; she was walking on the roof tiles
of my meagre brain due to lack of sleep –
you will believe me this time, I think.
My city, I tell you – that's not a lie.

I saw her last night late in the afternoon –
you don't believe me, I can tell and it's natural.
I saw her either in my sleep or in your wakefulness
and she was a gorgeous maiden lying on the beach.

I approached her cautiously – it's true –
fearing the god, who created her so beautiful.
She was sleeping serenely, and I thought I would sit beside her
while a diamond, which also found itself there,
was sparkling, blinding my eyes.

A peculiar sprout of my sleep's imagination!
It was like being in a room
where my exit was blocked by the diamond's rays
in such a way, that if they crossed my eyes,
I would surely be lost with the stamp of death.

How would I slip through such great danger?
"I shall wait a while", I said – "until dusk
to see what happens next". And what did I see?

The light, like a wakeful eye, was waiting there
knowing what a mouse I was, deep down.
I shall make an effort, I thought,
to escape quickly, from the side, like lightning.

While I was still upright it burnt my ribs
as the dawn light was reflected on me.
    And now, before I die,
listen to me, brothers and friends.
I saw my city sleeping on the beach.
(It seems she'd come down from the roof-tiles).
She was beautiful; like the girl of the olive grove,
and unbelievably sweet; an inexplicable thing.
Just imagine; centuries have passed
and in reality she should be heading
towards cruel old age and the silence of time.

I don't know how this miracle came about
neither can I carry on.
On this night, before the arrival of the song,
I shall sail out to distant pious places.
A night-flower is blossoming in my soul already …

The maiden will become youthful and gorgeous in the beauty of love,
when she begins to sound again.

    August 1980

BIRTH DATE OF A HORSE

Every time I feel tired
you materialise, – a deserted hovel, before me.
I spell out your name, a multifaceted yearning,
somewhat faded on the side facing the sun,
and little by little poisoned by the sea.

I remember your Greek High School
in tender years, on the sand. Suddenly
a voice full of mint and curious eyes:
"Sir, look what we found[17] while digging!"

They had a huge Turkish flag in their hands
and we took it to the Police.
They arrested it for further questioning
and they sent us home to sleep.

That's what I do now, I sleep
and I recall those years of the flag.

My eyes brimmed full of tears –
time is short, the receptacle is large –
as I rolled over a stone[18] it was covered in blood.

---

17 "Sir, look what we found": in 1968, the students of the Greek Gymnasium went for a walk to the seaside. They found a huge Turkish flag buried in the sand. The Principal handed it to the Police.

18 I rolled a stone: a cyclopean monolith found in the ancient cemetery of the Necropolis of Salamis; it was covering a burial of horses.

I found the horses hidden beneath their hides which had decomposed.

A little of Engomi and Salamis
still remained with a disturbed[19] statue in the sea.

The Italian man who had found it, suckled from
the eight breasts of the mother and the daughter
(a half-moon net in her hair)
and he handed it over to the invader.

I had to enjoy it at any cost.
And what did I do? I wrapped myself
in the red flag at night time, I took up a scimitar
and I left through the Famagusta gate.[20]
Then piercing the light – this is no lie –
I entered the Trojan camp.
Brave Diomedes had my back,
and next to him ingenious Odysseus.

At the border of the towns, at the monastery
of Apostle Varnavas,[21] I discard the red tunic
and I sneak among the horses.
Let me sleep too, with my sword beneath my cheek.
I entered an ancient tomb, that is, close to the horse's reins,
awaiting the time and the day that wasn't far off in coming,
judging by the light.

---

19   a disturbed statue: in 1980, an Italian tourist swimming near Salamis, found a statue of the goddess of fertility with many breasts. The statue was taken by the "Turkish-Cypriot Police".
20   Famagusta gate: the eastern gate of the Venetian Walls of Nicosia.
21   the monastery of Apostle Varnavas: this monastery is situated between Engomi and Salamis, near the horses' burial site. Apostle Varnavas' body (the founder of the Church of Cyprus) was buried in a Mycenaean temple found at that site.

My own note: When we say Trojans
we don't mean those much-afflicted people,
or Hecuba and Priam and Hector.
Those Trojans entered with us
among the horses of Engomi with their god Apollo.

August 1980

LESSON IN ARCHAELOGY

I should go to bed early to wake up early
to find myself with my city inside the waves –
no captain's commands and no screams;
secretly the good lovers of time, with raised knee
and a blow to both empty heads
we should say "It serves us right."

    Our multi-storeyed home was
limping and leaning over day by day
as we – especially I – were compiling works of art,
admiring books, cleaning the floor.

I – as this discourse is about me,
and not about all of you any longer –
I, who was an angel in the devil's hand
was being bad-mouthed,
while I kept silent
kissing them sourly in the morning
and before lunch at noon,
and three times in the evening.
That is me; while you wonder who I am.

At this point, the problem seems to be halfway solved.
The solution lies in the sand,
Beneath the god-shrouded torsos of the statues.

One day we went there (to the Tomb of Salamis[22])
accompanied by Dr Hatzioannou.[23]
There was a big swell in the sea.

He was smiling under his brimmed hat.
How could he imagine – and we, too, –
that in sixteen years' time (if that!)
we would be refugees carrying our bindles,
bandaging our wounds under carob trees
and under the Hesperides and the golden apples of Ormidia.[24]

Perhaps now it sounds funny my good friend, when you say
"I am holding onto life, so that I can live to complete my work"[25]
and I, in turn, contemplate the events that have come to pass.
I am thinking about the headless, stout and solitary
Roman statues in the gymnasium, watching from everywhere
a pointing finger – they say it was Attila's hand – we know that now,
but back then, you were revealing to us, while smiling widely,
that for a little while and for ever more – we had entered the city of Zeus,[26]
as we walked over the tomb
that hid river deities[27] and bay leaf orchards

---

22 The Tomb of Salamis: a tomb found at the ancient city of Salamis, covering a steam room and mosaics of the 3rd century AD.

23 Dr Hatzioannou: Philologist, Principal of the Famagusta Gymnasium, author of the study *Ancient Cyprus in Greek Sources*. In 1958 he took his students (including the poet) on an excursion to Salamis. That day he was wearing a hat and used a walking stick.

24 Ormidia: a village where many refugees from Famagusta settled. Quote from *Cyprus Today*, no. XII, no 3–4, May 1974, p. 67: "Christodoula, aged 70, from Famagusta, now under the orange tree in Sotira. She will die under the orange tree as she suffers from cancer."

25 I am holding onto life, so that I can complete my work: words written by Dr Hatzioannou to the poet in a letter in August 1980.

26 City of Zeus: according to Isocrates (Evagoras 12–18) and Tacitus (*Annales* III 62), Zeus of Salamis. arrived in Cyprus with the Achaeans.

27 River deities: mosaic showing the God River Eurotas, found in the Thermal Baths of Salamis (3rd century AD).

and tame animals and bows.
Time does know something too!

Don't be bitter, my beloved city.
Take water from the palm of my hand to quench your thirst,
take birds with which to fly,
take the sea to cool your brow
and wear a garland there,
so that I may see you.

   August 1980

CAULDRON

A huge cauldron[28] blocks your eyes
and a thousand roosters block your ears.
I am not speaking about your breasts and your four-pointed crosses –
inside the folds of foaming nectar.

It was then I saw the golden clasp at your waistline
huddled in the light with a semblance of sleep.
I saw lots more that I won't reveal
until the last judgement.
There the gnashing of teeth
will be a fine spectacle for loiterers.

But, my God, these people
have shown unbelievable tolerance and endurance to torture
in handing over the baton to these blissful, original cuckolds
in the words of Giorgos Philippou Pierides.[29]

What can I do for you now? What can I tell you?
Hail, Famagusta,
Salamis, Engomi, Stylli,
Spatharikon, Lefkonikon, Akanthou,
Rizokarpason, Tavrou, Aegialousa,

---

28   A cauldron: found in tomb 79, in the necropolis of Salamis (8th century BC). Similar cauldrons were found at Olympia, Delphi and Etruria. It is decorated with eight busts of griffins and four men-birds with two faces.

29   Giorgos Philippou Pierides: Founder and Director of the Public Library of Famagusta. In his book *O Kairos ton Olvion* (Athens, 1979) he writes: "the rich, with their erosive influence, suspended the healthy development of the place and they are not without responsibility for the disaster. Even today, we witness their remains cultivating their interests and their merriment on the devoured body of Cyprus."

Davlos, Acheritou, Lythragome,
Gastria, Voukolida –
these are only a few places on your eastern flank,
excluding the woodlands and the ravines
to avoid the straight road that takes us
to Morphou and Kyrenia
and other long-suffering Greek names.

The worm that wracks my insides is hunting
the miracle of the betrayed resurrection –
no, by Zeus, no! We should not exceed our limits for now;
remember the Furies.

Better hide the cauldron that we were talking about
at the start of our exorcism,
in great depths as big as your eyes,
let's sacrifice roosters to bond your breasts
fraternally with the light;
breasts of lightning in the unravelling of sleep.

Such a statue I have not seen anywhere
– not even in the courtroom of God –
with bats adorning its teeth,
in the rattles of its unburied admirers.

We've been speaking all this time and I haven't offered you
a coffee. I apologise.
I am off to bring it now. I won't be long.

And when I returned, what did I see?
The city had gone for a stroll in the mountains;
she could not wait even for two minutes.
Does she deserve love?

August 1980

BIRDS

"Liberate the city my birds";
this will be the code with a different response code:
"Liberate the city, chancellors of the intellect
and imbeciles of fashion."

Who can imagine these keys?
Tanks will be guarding the city all day
in case she awakens and slips through their fingers.
They have strict orders: "Shoot to kill,"
given this damn scarcity of flesh.
"But be careful," they told them. "The mortars
must avoid hitting stones and flowerbeds
because snakes, kept
for the bad times, could lash out
and then woe to us, the best of thieves.
As for you gentlemen of the armed forces,
be careful where you walk, and to whom you raise your hand
and the sinkers of your eyes, stolen from the fishermen
with such toil, blood and sacrifices,[30]
so that they don't all go to waste."

These roughly were the words of the chief pirate,
whose one eye was hidden out of frugality
while the other one was borrowed.

---

30   blood and sacrifices: during the first anniversary of the Turkish invasion of Cyprus, the leader of the Turkish-Cypriots asked the "fighters" not to return an inch of the land taken by the Turkish army with "blood and sacrifices" as he called it.

You could witness many such things.

Now then, my birds, as we were saying,
the code is: "Liberate the city my birds".
Who would imagine that you …

I have laid out my plan with every beak
from your beaks, every feather
from your feathers, every talon
from your shining, delicate, infallible talons.

Woe to those high up in their tanks!
But don't forget the response code:
"Liberate the city, chancellors of the intellect
and imbeciles of fashion."
Because, if in your stubbornness and the holy dance
of the reaper's onward charge,
you get drunk on the landmines and corpses,
and you lose track of the time to return,
or lamely climb on a bell-tower or minaret,
shouting to me "What's the response code?"
The response code, eh?
Have you been so misled then?
What were we saying?
Are you chancellors of the intellect
or imbeciles of fashion? Damn it!

August 1980

COLTS AND HORSES

«Κέλητι τελείω» [A perfect horse]
                              Ariston, son of Nikon[31]

Famagusta, I am returning, riding on a colt –
don't ask where I found it or it found me.
This is how things happened:
I climbed down from a sycamore tree like Zaccheus,
I jumped over a river, I stepped on a key
and here I am now – on a colt,
under the palm leaves, with children watching me
from the palm trees that they have climbed, wearing gloves.

My colt stops for a while,
turning its head left to eat dried thistles.
It eats, looking at ease like Makarios.[32]
The road is long, almost two hundred metres,
and the colt must have strength – not like that mule
– Muhammad's aunt[33] with her luminous neck, was riding it on rugs –
which stumbled, I don't know how, when she was looking silently
at the salt of the Salt-Lake.
"You die as well!"

---

31   Ariston, son of Nikon: on an inscription in ancient Athens: "With an adult race-horse; Ariston, son of Nikon from Karpasia of Cyprus".

32   Makarios: Archbishop and primate of the autonomous Greek Orthodox Church of Cyprus, and the first President of the Republic of Cyprus from 1960 to 1977.

33   Muhammad's aunt: Umm Haram: it is believed that Umm Haram, the aunt of the prophet Muhammad, died at the Salt-Lake, in Larnaca, Cyprus, after falling from her mule; she was entombed there in a mosque.

The two of us, the colt and the man from Famagusta
(Ariston, son of Nikon from Karpasia)
will certainly go as far as Djanbulat Gate[34]
with the buried wheat and barley
inside the storeroom next to the Customs House.
Look at what happened to the Venetians now,
great artisans,[35] architects, engineers,
who had set up their terrible, merciless machine
slaughtering countless conquerors.

Djanbulat the Turk, – brave lad, – gets angry,
charges with his horse and in the heat of the moment
he smashes into the machine.
– Sword, heart, head, were cut into a thousand pieces.
It's not so bad for him as he was made a hero
and from his blood a big fig tree sprang up above the gate
and the Turkish women who had no children
drank the milk sap from the figs with the hope – here's hope –
of bearing male children brave like him.

The wheat, the barley and the fig tree,
the Venetians, Djanbulat, the Customs House,
cover a span of four hundred years
but add another three to be precise.

What a miracle! While science and humanity
gallop further towards new skies
and new conquests – here's a conquest! –

---

34 Djanbulat was a Turkish military officer who was killed by a Venetian war machine during the Ottoman siege of Famagusta in 1571. Famagusta was under Venetian rule from 1489 to 1571 AD. Djanbulat Gate was named after him by the Ottoman conquerors; it is a gate on the Venetian fort of Famagusta, opposite the Customs House.

35 great artisans: the Venetians built the walls of Famagusta with great artisanship. The architects of the walls, Nicolo Foscarini (1482) and Nicolo Prioli (1496) became famous for these exceptional structures.

the Turkish men and women charge forward again.
Mothers mourn the children they lose,
and the men – men who were once
in Djanbulat's memory
slaughter the body of Cyprus once again,
so slender like a Cypress tree,
they smash it to smithereens.

Well then, what should I do now? This is the point
I wanted to reach and here's my mule.

Good mule, bitter mule, blessed mule,
born twelve centuries before Christ.
Walking on furrowed soil, covering
oil lamps and troughs and bathtubs
and hand-mills, engraved ornaments,
weights of handlooms, projectiles of slingshots,
fishing sinkers and many seashells
with bulls and birds and a rooster painted on them
and I can see a goat and a horse as well.
With loving adoration,
the mule goes past the city of copper
near the Salt-Lake – the salt thickens, the dawn breaks
and I, like a Mycenaean sword, like a Cypress tree,
(the tree ringing with birds),
swim in a sea of happiness.

Between the meteorite of Umm Haram
and the star-studded moon crescent of Djanbulat,
my mule and I discard the covers of sadness
smiling at the glorious donkeys that carry loads of salt –
loads of thick salt.

August 1980

TO ALMIGHTY GOD

To almighty God
Kypris
makes a vow
for her child Kypris
                Inscription at Amathus[36]

The Greek Wing Commander[37] looked them in the eye
and said to them "You almost saw us.
Don't you believe me; we were ready to come
in the nick of time. I know what I'm talking about."

His words were muffled by the horses
of hundreds of Cypriot soldiers.
Applause was optional.

"… As for the reason we didn't come,
let's leave it for another time –
when we get another chance."

To almighty God
Kypris
makes a vow
for her child Kypris

---

36   Amathus: Amathus was one of the oldest royal cities of ancient Cyprus. Its ancient cult of Aphrodite was the most important, after Paphos, in Cyprus.

37   Greek Wing Commander: an actual person.

At the mouth of the River of Fire
we sat on the soft grass
and smeared honey on our wounds.
There, on a night, like tonight,
a night of refuge,
we hung up our guitars, blood dripping from their necks
like the moon emptying some barley from its bags
willing or not it becomes delirious and is gnawed by fear.

Ah but, the cause is not so sad
and awkward as at first,
neither does the heart tolerate seeing
the barley rotting in the field.

> *To almighty God*
> *Kypris*
> *makes a vow*
> *for her child Kypris*

Somewhere, time weighs heavily, and it swells
and overturns in the spray
of the ghastly sea made up of milk
and dreadful soil and angry planks.

As I detoured, I entered such a residence
and put in many plants to keep me in tune
and I called on good, migratory birds
and I placed a ring on their imperious beak[38]
and a handful of arrows in their sharp claws[39]
and I said "look at the Constellation of the Swan

---

38   a ring on their imperious beak: birdlike-women idols of the later Copper Era, with a Near-Eastern influence, at the Cyprus Archaeological Museum.

39   arrows in their sharp claws: cf. the emblem of the USA.

and that of the Bear, of the Great Dog and of Ophiuchus".[40]
They didn't need another word. They surged forward
like pebbles being dragged by a river over a waterfall
and the moon was filling out day and night
until they arrived above the city.

There they made their circular formations
with the accuracy of a Russian Olympiad
and then, they surged at the ship of the sun.

People might think that I am exaggerating,
or that birds ripped up the sky,
people might think anything.
Who would know that each city looks like a ship that lies precious
and abandoned in "the suspicion of sleep" and of white death.

A spider's web covers the city
from end to end like a stretched rope
at Moscow's City Council, at the forty pancakes.[41]

Birds build nature in a peculiar manner
starting from its other side.
But with these birds, I don't think
you have a problem; the only thing they ask for
is a warm place to lay their eggs
and then, farewell.

> *To almighty God*
> *Kypris*
> *makes a vow*

---

40 Ophiuchus: serpent bearer. Nicaenetus of Samos, a Greek epic and epigrammatic poet (3rd century BC), calls Cyprus, "Ophiodea", serpent country.

41 forty pancakes: A. Chekov's *Three Sisters*, Act 2: "FERAPONT. In Moscow, a contractor told us only yesterday at the council, some merchants had pancakes to eat. One of them ate forty pancakes, and they say he died."

for her child Kypris

I had a little surplus money
so, I sent them to the city that I love.
I ordered some silk[42] from there
and I have at my disposal, a thousand rolls.

Well, gentlemen, I am beginning to believe
that life, however short and precious,
did not come unexpectedly.
We were all waiting for it.
Who at present, or later, or never,
will learn to step over it, and not only that.

The water we wash life with, the dye we paint it with,
the blood and tears with which we often adorn it,
grow old with it and dissipate in its chest.
And what remains from all this? What else
except for the end of the poem and the city somewhere over there.

September 1980

---

42   silk: during the Frankish and Venetian Rule of Cyprus (1191–1571 AD), the silk of Cyprus was famous for its exceptional quality.

BEGINNING OF THE INDICTION[43]

We all know who Pnytagoras[44] is
or we could find out –
(they say he was the King of Salamis) –
but, Pnytagoras Street, my little Pnytagoras Street,
between the Holy Cross and the Holy Belt,
is known by me and me alone. Woe to me:
I envy the rats of this street,
the stray dogs, the wild tomcats
as they come from Acropolis Street and go down
towards the junction of Pentelis and Ilarionos Streets
ending up in my Pnytagoras – lucky lads!

I wish I were the female rat of my house,
the stray dog that enters my yard
and the wild tomcat that opens the fridge
to find its forgotten piece of chicken.

Even if I were the snake and the nettle,
the tree that died, the broken door,
the exhausted precious amaranthus
that lies down to sleep in a spider's webs.

September 1980

---

43   Indiction: a Christian church calendar year. The Indiction in the Orthodox Church begins on 1 September.

44   Pnytagoras: a king (351–332 BC) of the ancient Greek city-state of Salamis in Cyprus. He was the nephew and successor of Evagoras II, who was overthrown in 351 BC and exiled due to his pro-Persian stance.

GOOD FRIDAY

And since the city was slaughtered
while falling asleep on her wings,
what do I do, as I watch them wipe off
her salty blood, rhesus O positive?

Immediately, without wasting any time
I take off, full of inspiration like a panther,
charging at the chains.
I was lucky to miss their barbs
but what do I see from high above?
The city wandering over another city,
their blood mixing and piling up to such a point
that you couldn't distinguish mother Morphou
from Kyrenia or Famagusta.
And you couldn't name this or that country town;
they were none and all of them.

What the devil? Something is happening here.
A mismatched and disorderly love is born.
I wipe the sweat from my wings,
I dim the light and I dig
into the breast of the beast – and again I lose you:

You were here, opposite Lebanon,
you were picking your nose[45] with your finger

---

45   picking your nose: the shape of Cyprus at one end is shaped like a nose, that is, the Karpasia Peninsula.

and now you have taken up another place;
you have been exchanged with another island[46] on the map –
human mistakes.

According to the same logic, I search but cannot find you
on the home soil where I lost you – such a big city
with a proper plan, hotels, public parks –
where has she gone? Who is acting as her doppelgänger?

What ram, or other sacrificial offering now sprouts in place of Isaak,
Iphigenia and other martyrs of the theatre?

I do not know what to say or what to presume.

But it is clear; a city from time immemorial
a mythical city, was suddenly robbed of its voice,
and was shackled.
If only I could have been deep in the well of her eye
the moment when her innermost core
was being sealed with a mixture
of congealed and callous sludge of dejection and rupture.
Something could have been done:
The odd things are few, the futilities are excessive
and the detail is complete.
I could have saved her, taking from her hand
the silver plaque with the inscription that said "FAMAGUSTA".
I could have secretly hidden her name in my bosom while
pretending to be looking out of the window.

I have learnt these tricks through my multifaceted adoration
of your history's fate, most beautiful motherland.
I don't claim to be a know-all; they've stolen my knowledge

---

[46] exchanged you with another island: in a European Council journal *Forum2/80*, the designer made a mistake and placed Cyprus where Crete is on the map.

that filled my innards during the last uprising.
Now only the key remains; the magical little key;
if I lose it I am lost, I find it and I am found by it,
you, an unkempt city with a thousand masters
and I, a novice of sight and a nail in your heart.

Don't fear, don't grieve and don't despair.
While I embroider you with loving adoration
for seven generations I will protect you from the custodians.

Your little blood-soaked body
will lean on the uncompromising and spoilt
song of the nymph. You are surrounded by graces,
flyers of the resurrection and erotic guitars.

September 1980

THE PERFECT CARBON

At the base of half of the world's diamonds
I slapped you my poor city, woe!
Perhaps your world turned up-side-down
and you came into my arms betrayed.

Luckily, I had with me a dictionary
of an effective benevolent revolution
and I indicated silently to you
that you are innocent.

Only you tore your shoes a little
attempting to outrun Death.
Life's gains were yours
and Death took your discarded veil[47]
and entered your unlocked home.

It was a hot August; the cicadas
on the tips of lemon leaves were preparing for
your return from the fields.

You, full of diamonds, crocuses[48] and myrtles,
propelled by the sea breezes and the waves
with a little bag under your armpit
and with chest ailments, had arrived.

---

47 your fallen veil: see the Roman mosaics of Paphos, Cyrpus depicting Thisbe and Pyramus in the House of Dionysus, Paphos (3rd century AD).

48 crocuses … waves: see the Homeric Hymn to Aphrodite, 7th century BC.

Smiling you sowed flowers
with the songs of a thousand dead.

Meaning they are poorly made and frigid
bearing their own testimony
of future afflictions and sorrows.

Where the cheap bracelet
and the worthless bead of light sparkle,
gallows are erected for the guilty
but, by mistake, they take the uneducated,
the fallacy and deception and betrayal.

Consequently, stripped of your best offspring
who wither seeing you thus,
you wrap yourself in vile grass
with the bloom of revulsion and celestial eunuchs,
you attempt to recite the poem of humiliation,
to cry once more in my arms,
here, take this hiding; take that too,
and that!
Take pounds and coins too.

At the root of half the world's diamonds
I adorned you, golden wayward city.
I hid you in the dark, and placed you in a sack
high in the attic, and not a word to anyone…

To the churches we will proudly take cushions
stuffed with olive leaves.[49]

---

49   full of olive leaves: on Palm Sunday, in Cyprus, the faithful take to church a sack
     full of olive leaves to be blessed and kept there until Pentecost Sunday.

We will then leave making sure our shadow
doesn't fall on the road; Aladdin's magic lamp.

Whole days and nights I sit and ponder
where to scatter the blue ash.

Secretly, I go to the trough, in the middle of the city square.

Suddenly the chiming of a clock stops me, streams of time
in my capillary blood, in the mauve temptation.

I run to escape and I hide somewhere
in a heavy, hard place.
This is the pendant of the city
and your breasts are like those of a rotten gazelle.[50]

I know that I still have a long way to go,
to empty the moon and fill many buckets,
to pull out the dried thorn from the light.

Stones of time, dust from the pulverised
tongue of the snake, the tooth of Alexander.
Divine spears, wide-winged wayfarers,
vain hopes for unformed carbon.

September 1980

---

50   your breasts are like those of a rotten gazelle: from *Song of Songs*, 4:5.

FOR THE CITY THAT REMAINED FAITHFUL TO HER COMRADES

Dressed in her sinful costume
with imprints of trees and birds
she sleeps beside the power of her name.

With the sand of sleep in her hair
she calms the dreams and the bodies
of the morning statues.
Snakes caress her breasts.[51]

What has she to lose? She cares so little
about Death's willow[52] and the verdant swords?[53]

In a little while the tray will be full of ash
and the flame of her face, erstwhile sacred,
will wash her wound with cotton wool.

The edge of her eye becomes salty.
Her dress melts in the dormitory.

---

51 Minoan goddess with snakes.
52 Shakespeare, *Othello*: Desdemona's sad willow song, Act 4, Sc. 3.
53 Othello's words: "Keep up your bright swords, for the dew will rust them." Act 1, Sc. 2.

She was a breath of fresh air in the early years,
now she lies motionless in the heart of the fish.[54]

If you are coming from afar, please,
shake off the rain from your hair
and I will know who you are.

September 1980

54　in the heart of the fish: Matthew 12:39 "and no sign will be given to it but the sign of the prophet Jonah"; Matthew 12:40 "For just as *Jonah* was in the *belly* of that great sea-monster for *three days* and *nights*, so will the *Son* of *Man* be in the *heart* of the *earth* for *three days* and *nights*."

HEADLESS STATUE

I hear your head has been taken
to Constantinople as a holy relic.
Gallant Byzantine emperors have placed you
in the red and gold.
The star of God's Saint Sophia Church
studies you and covers you.
And you, a woman, in a late hour,
open your closed eyelids.
You look for us in vain; we are away
on a journey and you beckon us "come to my dorm."
But, beautifully sculptured head,
we are looking for the rest of your body,
in a city that resembles you.
If we succeed we shall say this bone is ours.

Unfortunate city, lying in bed sick for ten years,
a lampstand without a lamp,
headless and cold like lead.

Let me not see you and get upset, my precious one.
I know you are missing; it's all well-known.
Your skull is in a huge box
decorated with streamers and little stars
all made of paper, seeds of bravery,
it travelled the world to be bestowed
from cabarets and brothels
in the sky of the city that used to reign.

Don't think badly of me, all of you who hear me.
All these things serve the actual memory of mortals
and all the rest, the cleansing of memory.

September 1980

THE HULL OF A SHIP

The city of carnations was abandoned
in the hull of the ship,[55]
infatuated, and ready to jump ashore.

A thick knife slashes the sea in two.
Like a swift bird with sandals in the countryside,
a boat has brought urchins to the wind.

And a bronze colt
is deep in the soil of the earth.

I saw the snake and it looked like a winged horse
and a winged woman.
She too, was made of metals that fall in the deep sea.
The sound of a motorcycle reaches the fish.

Can you believe it Nicolaides?[56]
The soul drowns in the shallows
and in the depths, it sinks –
with a small sail on the heart
and broad sunlight on the silver olive tree
of the archipelago.

---

55   Hull of a ship: cf. Homer, *The Iliad*, A 26, 'κοίλαι νῆες' (hollow ships). And in *The Odyssey*, 8: f507, 'κοίλον δόρυ', hollow timber (the Trojan Horse).
56   Nicolaides: the author Nicos Nicolaides (1885–1956) had close bonds with Famagusta.

Her hair rinses her feet with myrrh,
her eyes warm the most ancient forehead
that touches with crossed arms
the edge of the flower garden
smiling at the photographer.

The ribbon on the edge of her apron,
her collar a circle of innocence
and you wish you were born
in her era, that of the swallow.

In the distribution, you wish such a girl
could fall to you
with the harbour and the perfume jar
of the main road of return.

Oh, to sleep all night in open tombs with her hair loose
whispering in Cypro–Syllabic[57]
the appropriate grace from the ship's hull
that folds itself over her.

July/October 1980

---

[57] The Cypro-Syllabic script is a system of writing with a syllabic character; it was used in Cyprus between the mid-11th century BC and the end of the 2nd century BC.

THE ELEMENT OF WATER

While I was watering the garden
an angel descended
and sat on the stone with wings tucked in.

Luckily, as I was absorbed in my work,
I did not notice his presence
and I almost splashed him.
(A few drops wouldn't matter of course).

I greeted him as the birds
greet their neighbour. "He must have come to drink water,"
I whispered to my ear, when,
disdainfully, he left, dancing in the wind.

I threw a bucket at him angrily
and I got him right on the head.

Approaching with a barrelled shotgun in my hands
and a hunter's flask and smart boots
I watched him crawling in the bushes.

"You wretch!" I called out to him, "What are you trying to do?"
I loaded and fired; the shots
spread here and there, as though the target
was in the periphery and not in the centre.

•

This reminded me of the airborne parachutists,
falling like rain from the sky
in the villages of Mia Milia[58] and Hamit Mandres,
where haphazardly armed
and begging desperately for permission to shoot,
we were firing at them.
In their orange silk parachutes
they were descending and hiding
from the hollow and futile bullets
of the Pan-Hellenes.

How betrayal embellishes the hand
with a worthless nature and scattered marble statues!

Only one parachutist, blown by a mistake of the wind
in the wrong direction, remained between the two villages
and the debauchery of the guns from both sides.
He dragged himself to a thorny bush at the trunk of an olive tree.

I was reminded of all these by the angel
whom I had met in times of peace.
He would have remained lying
where the wind gathers piles of leaves,
if I didn't have the intuition to escape
and hide behind the fence – myself.

He came up to me, grabbed me from behind
and shouted "Fool, look how you made me bleed."
From his cast iron head
he took out a crimson cauliflower.
"Come with me now and learn a lesson."

---

58 Mia Milia and Hamit Mandres: villages next to Nicosia from where Turkish parachutists began the invasion of Cyprus on 20 July 1974.

Like a bird turning a deaf ear to the pathetic pleas
of the poacher "Don't, don't please"
and to the pleas of the land
"I give you this and that and those two mountains"
but in vain, in vain; that's how we arrived in the city of my forefathers.

What do you know of her, he asks tersely.
I replied with parts of the national anthem
"I recognise you from the appearance"
I added "and from the sword's cutting edge"[59]
I mess things up.

He drops me like a tortoise shell[60]
and I fall on a stony river bank.
I get up, and, limping, I head for
the deserted tailor's shop. I knock on the door.

I wanted a bit of shirt and pants,
painkillers, flavin, band aids.
All I found is a city completely naked,
hidden in the bushes like Odysseus,
her whole body trembling in the winter's claws.

I had not seen her so feverish,
unkempt, without sandals, without a rifle.
The trees around her formed a chorus
while she was abandoned in a heap.

---

59 "I recognise you from the appearance ... cutting edge": reference to the Greek national anthem. Its lyrics are: "I recognise you by the sharpness, of your fearsome sword, I recognize you by the gleam (in your eyes) with which you rapidly survey the earth. From the sacred bones, of the Hellenes arisen, and strengthened by your antique bravery, hail, o hail, Liberty!"

60 He drops me like a tortoise shell: reference to the legend that Aeschylus was killed by the fall of a tortoise from the claws of an eagle. "But notwithstanding all his precautions, Aeschylus was killed by the fall of a tortoise-shell, which, descended by the claws of an eagle high in the air, struck him on the head and broke his skull." *Pataphysica 2: Pataphysica E Alchimia*, Vol. 2.

Then I forgot all my sorrows;
I caressed her, and I lost myself in the water of the harbour,
all heart and chest.

I knew then, that in a few years' time, a unique,
sensitive angel – a tear of a nightingale –
would fall into my hands, and I, the fish
strangled by my old antics,
would mend my thoughts and deeds.

October 1980

THE VOICE OF BLOOD

Following on from the angel and his wings,
we, the Greeks, wanderers as usual,
shall snuff out the light of our voice
at the wind's sunset in the palm trees.

Those of you who find it difficult to understand,
let them replace the voice with a little blood.

Blood brings night and the stars
rise and fall
to alleviate some of the city's pain.

Her breath pierces my heart
and her memory gnaws at me like gnawing a rusk.

Beloved city, it has been years
since I last saw you, since we last met.

Your scent was like that of orange blossom;
the truth was as strong as the fragrance of the tree.
I always embraced you with such fervour, my dear one,
that I would die for you if I could bring back your large breasts of sand
before they spoilt you
and you became Venus and Hesperia[61]
and other hotels in the avenue.

---

61   Venus and Hesperia: two of the fifty-eight hotels of Famagusta in 1974.

The abscess of the sea preceded
the neurotic scene of chaining the shoreline.
The council workers were measuring urea, bacteria,
swift boats menaced the floating heads of the swimmers.

Carefree times and times of peace,
how discernible your tracks are in the soil!

Hell's depth increases with just one drop
of salty water; seawater or tears.

An old story poured again into the depth of thought
and in the mud of the long-awaited day of return.

When the tanks' tracks will be broken in half
like watermelons, cantaloupes and consecrated bread,
and the blood goes back into the vessel of the body
and the wings will be secured firmly around the armpits with wax.

November 1980

A MAGICAL GAME

I dread the thought that birds may cease
to knot their ties on the trees.
I dread to form their voice
in my ear piece, in case it suddenly ends.

And all these for your sake my little one.
With their help, I conjure you.
You count by five to one hundred
and then run to find us hiding all around.
We manage to shout: "Fair go for all"
and you start over, chasing us
all in a magical game.

Oh, birds and trees and stars,
I tremble lest you hide my city from my view.
Don't reveal her whereabouts, please,
let her go searching for her group of friends.
And when she finds it
she will cut the navel of the earth with scissors
and she will smile.

Alas, you assemble her
among many fragments of various kinds.
One day, in her mass grave[62] you found
the hand of a child, and on another day – its head.

---

62 mass grave: "The grass was removed, and the corpses of a woman and three men were uncovered in a mass grave, at Saint Memnon, Famagusta", *Days of Wrath in Cyprus*, 1975, pp. 126–7.

You assemble her and you identify her.
The limbs of ancient colossi are scattered;

I fear, we must look for them
in foreign galleries …

The Louvre[63] Museum and that of Berlin,
the London Museum, the Metropolitan, that of Vienna,
the Seraglio[64] Museum and that of Adana.

Cursed tomcats of an old spinster[65]
you soil the places of our beautiful city.

Girl, be patient and I shall assemble you.
Can't you see that I am struggling with my faith as collateral
to maintain those roots that I won't change
with anything in this world or any other world?

November 1980

---

63 Louvre Museum … Vienna: some of the museums holding precious ancient treasures of Cyprus
64 Seraglio: in the Turkish-Cypriot suburb of Seraglio and in the city of Adana, in Turkey, the Greek-Cypriot hostages were taken prisoners during the Turkish invasion of Cyprus in 1974.
65 an old spinster: Old Albion, is the old name for the UK a "guarantor power" of the Republic of Cyprus.

TOWARDS TRACHEA[66]

And the mountain which happened to be the target
had a golden locket around its neck
and a huge ball in its teeth and other instruments of the devil.

There is no way this Great Boulder
would change its faith. It managed to evade
Michael Angelo's[67] searching gaze;
only a Pope knows how the Great Sculptor
would transform the mountain's enslaved parts.

And since it slipped away from the hammer's threat,
it displays its bloodied outstretched hand
for the few of us who remain, to view it from above.

It knows us well, and its crumpled peak
releases an eagle from its corpse.
The greatly aged beast's hoof still has an iron toe.
As it bends it calls out with its two limestone horns[68]
"You can't defeat the Great Mountain by force."

Hell! That's right! Force is annihilated
under the stare of its master.

---

66 "Trachea": an area in the Karpasia Peninsula of Cyprus; now under Turkish occupation.
67 "Michael Angelo": in 1505 AD Pope Julius II asked Michael Angelo to build a tomb for him; the sculptor saw a mountain and wanted to turn it into a colossus; he was not allowed to do it.
68 lime stone horns: sacred horns to prevent evil, found in an ancient temple (12th century BC) in Cyprus.

Let's not insist then. This is the message
from the mountain that it saw with its own eyes
and fitted it in its wide nostrils
and sent it via Eos[69] who was hidden in the fields –
towards the city which was expecting thunderbolts.

Just imagine! In a summer month!
Doesn't summer show respect
towards the rain from the storm in a bright sky?
Suddenly everything escapes from the lid
of the Great Steam;[70] that's why we bow
to God's wishes,
with joyous birds on the ascent of the sky's expanse.
– His sleeves produce great numbers of pigeons
that fill the valleys with feathers and stalactites.

And you gaze and contemplate and lord it over
the city (that city again!) that has swelled around the infertile
foothills of the mountain like an overused ball,
tortured by the weight of forgetfulness,
with the three nails in the middle of a crazy love – yours and ours.

You have already consumed her,
you have channelled her into your bloodstream,
you encircle her from the spot where the sun's crescent
can be seen, like a dream by order;
a moon that was waning by moving its hand,
at the time that the sun was setting from the right side of the land
and the moon from the left side, kissing the shore.

November 1980

---

69   Eos: Goddess of Dawn, in Greek mythology.
70   Great Steam: Sanskrit; steam = soul.

SUBMISSION

The sun has fainted a long while ago
his weakened limbs no longer hold him up.
A wave thrown on the sand is surrendering
its last breath to the moon.

Deputy Chief! Present birds!
Tie the hands of our angel, behind his back.

Tarata tam! Revellers listen:
The lie is a tightrope-walker, the dream is a sleep-walker
and the footprint of shame is the night; remaining hidden in a veil
while stripping bare all the members
of the entourage heading to the mountain of shining light.

This is roughly what the ultra-glorious one was saying
examining the city's cheek
that was nestled in the trees and in the south wind.

With a pocket knife, he'd carve
her name on a telegraph pole,
keeping the bark for her initials,
he'd make a heart with two arrows
embedded in the ground; then he'd raise his eyes.

All is well, despite the bitterness
caused by his numerous fractures – a procession
of the Epitaph in the streets; harmonious sounds.

War rises up on crutches from the ruins
like a brother of the sun.

A procession of a dead man with his children
adorns the empty cells[71] of the island.

The tallest neck, ties the end
to the sinker of the year and is cast
deep in the body of infinite time,
where fire resides without a large opening
and it measures the sky inside
the whirlpool of his innards.

Fortunate deceased, who, using your own volition
could resurrect yourselves
thanks to the achievements of your forefathers.
The gift of life has already submitted to you.

November 1980

---

71   cells: found at the Necropolis of the ancient Greek city of Salamis in Cyprus. They were tombs for common mortals.

THE ANGRY SUN

In my homeland where the sun rises at midnight,
and the moon is born in the morning
the faces of the city dwellers are like funerary lilies
while those of the villagers are like wine[72] and rusks.

I will not add any other information;
sin weighs heavily on my people,
delineating their art, their words and their statues,
their political science, their everyday sacrifice.

Melons, potatoes, pumpkins,
cucumbers and tomatoes are sold cheaply.

My homeland is full of multivitamins
and antibiotic honey for immunity.
And yet here, with its prickly pears –
a natural barrier against evil –
its canes resilient to injustice –
the land is withering in the sorrow of shame
which a poet judge – a chef of virtue –
is concocting in his workshop.
In the jug he places many herbs
and grafts his wild gaze onto the fire.

---

72 "the villagers are like wine": in Cyprus, after a burial, the family of the dead person offers bread or rusks, wine, olives and cheese. It symbolises consolation.

This gentleman – if he is not a portrait –
is like me a little – in spirit –
while he simultaneously possesses some of my habits –
benevolence, humour, piety, love,
isolation owing to his frankness,
a feeling of responsibility, honesty.

I am not speaking about me, I'm talking about all of you
the way you will become in years to come.
As for me, forget me, I am spent,
whatever I had to give, I gave it. I am dying…

And upon his death
lilies bend over him (first stanza),
and wine is poured and rusks.

Pretences and kowtowing follow.
Public expenses and cheap tomatoes.
No one believed him or listened to him.
They weep for him with crocodile tears,
synthetic, voluntary, premeditated.
Even their handkerchief is artificial.

Only his old childhood city with her little plaits
stands by him in death splendidly
anointing him with the holy oil of her name.

December 1980

THE THIRD DIMENSION

The female-producing men[73]
those who produce girls
in the whole island (six hundred names)
came and lined up in front of the city: workers, drug merchants, thugs,
professionals of many kinds, village presidents, policemen,
ogling the city. If they had set foot on her soil first
they would have filled up the city with girls.

Many male-producing men also came – horror! –
Those who left their jobs and ran to this place
so the city would not think that Cyprus is a pawn of sucklings.

They came grinding their teeth and
sporting glorious moustaches – what a paradox!
And among those strong bodies, there were some milksops,
and some spineless men, advancing and baying for a sacrifice.

On the other side, female-producing men were boasting
that they had their own Hector and Diomedes,
their Prometheus and their Alexander the Great.

•

The proponents of male-producing men claimed that
they had Achilles, the crafty Odysseus,
Hercules, Laocoön and Ajax.

---

73 "The female-producing men … the male producing men": When Cyprus became an independent republic in 1960, the population split into two political groups: the supporters of President Makarios and the supporters of General Grivas. This was followed by the creation of the terrorist organisation EOKA B and the subsequent military coup.

You'd think the clash would have been unavoidable
if some producers of both genders had not intervened.
They brought with them their boys and girls
the same number of women, the tombs of their ancestors.

We guarantee, they said, that we will all go
to this city that lies opposite.
Leave your antics aside for other times.
Your children, females and males
are god's creations, wind and rain.
Unless with the passing of the years, science will
predetermine storms and floods
and immobilize the light of the sun
juxtaposing its own formula.

It's a shame then that we subject ourselves
to physical barriers; that we don't control
every molecule that grows on the planet –
look at the city, it is in agony; let her not be absent
from any home or table.

At the end of these words the leaders were teary.
They shook hands wrapped up in the rags
of the freezing wind.[74] They strapped on their bundle
of return, caressed their offspring's hair,
got into the cars smothered in a cloud of laughter,
on the meandering road, that joins one city with another,
they opened the shutters of eternity and turned on the radio.

If you ask, Television starts when the sun sets
while testing its last leap of death into the sea.

December 1980

74 "wrapped up in the rags of the freezing wind": after the failure of the Nazi winter invasion of the Soviet Union, the Germans retreated during the winter time, suffering many loses.

THE RISE FROM SLEEP

Birds, full of bitter almonds,
stare you straight in the eye,
your silent lips quiver, you pull up the blanket.

The hills invested with guarding posts recede,
the Turkish guns turn yellow
and their weapons disintegrate – scrap metal.

Five pounds will buy a tank hatch
fifteen will buy tank tracks.

Let's not talk about these anymore. They are in the past.
We are still preparing to forget
the city of our dreams,
like a child breaks an almond and finds a bitter kernel.

In my homeland, this happens often.
Cities are given up to premonitions
and they roll downhill on bicycles.

An old car that's been killed
extends the silence. With trembling lips
the wind explores the leaves of the south wind
and the rooster begins the golden coins.

•

From her grandfather, the city inherited
a good life, euthanasia and tamed stone.

The latter brings the city to a pilgrimage
of her venerable temple; she digs with her nails
to bring out the harmonious messages
of the statues that sleep in the deep
layers of the earth – What a city!
Once upon a time she exhibited those statues
in bazaars smiling wholeheartedly.

I won't be biased towards the city.
The city is lost, why should I care?

Only – permit me a couple of words –
before I enclose the carnation in its bud
and the crow turns white, I'll also tell you this:

The eyes see whatever
is an optical illusion.
All the rest are kept
in the memory of the Gods.

You and I, the two of us, one person's figure,
we don't study the heart of a swan,
we don't break the stone, we don't utter air.
We are the counterweights who walk around the periphery
as they encircle us in a hideously barbaric manner.[75]

A chicken that smiles upon the beast of love
is led astray by the monster of horror
for the great country of yours[76] – where does it lie?
A flea on His head and nothing else, are we,
the damned of the earth.

---

75 as they encircle us in a hideously barbaric manner: Turkey is 72 km from Cyprus, placing under its dominion the northern part of Cyprus.

76 the great country of yours: the invasion of Cyprus in 1974, by Turkey, was made possible with weapons from the NATO alliance.

But take heart, the time is near, even now,
when you will own a chair and table again.
Oh, sullen and silly people, you will also have
the light that springs from hope
that emanates from His crazy cap.

December 1980

ENDEAVOUR

The famous[77] city
made her decision;
She bared her chest,
walked to the window
– opened that too –
and she received two cannonballs to the heart.

Women came with the rhythm
of a great stage director.
They mourned her, embracing her cheeks.
She passed away almost peacefully, as they said,
and they tipped her out into the next room.

Here the dream is cut …
Now I am descending along a broken road
as tufts of grass grow immensely.
Now I am walking towards the sea shore
with all the stars above the land.

I look at my watch. Two thousand years
have passed, and the place has seen
no progress. We enter a lemon-yellow zone;
the leaves gurgle
and medusa's hair plaits the sea breeze.

---

77 The famous city: see *Recital concerning the sweet land of Cyprus, entitled 'Chronicle'* by Leontios Machairas (1380–1450 AD). "My aim is to create fame for this sacred island, and while I do that, I won't write any lies". Published by R. M. Dawkins, Oxford, 1932.

•

We have time another two thousand years
to decide about this city.
It's time therefore to take certain measures:
Take up adzes and picks to demolish
the invisible wall raised soundlessly
by a bad Fate while we slept.
With trumpets and icons of litany,
with a belt[78] made of string,
with the holy cross thrown in the sea[79] and such practices
we will melt the flint in the wall
to make it prominent.
And then, we will all charge over it
with ladders, spears, banners,
with lit torches and crossbows
we shall get into its treasure chests – wealth and glory!

This, then, is the city that I ask you
to take away from this corner.
I will reveal her name to you
at the end of your endeavour.

January 1981

---

78 a belt made of string: for protection against calamities (drought, deaths, etc.) in Cyprus they "tie" the church with a string, like a belt wrapped around it, after a vigil.

79 the holy cross thrown in the sea: During the Feast of the Holy Theophany (Epiphany), each year on 6 January, the tradition has been the tossing of a cross into the water to be retrieved by divers. The Feast commemorates the Baptism of Christ and the divine revelation of the Holy Trinity.

THE TRUNK TREMBLES

The trunk trembles in Regina's[80] heart,
the tree leaves tremble amongst the pigeons
and the breath trembles on the lips.

A loud voice, hidden
like a snake under a skull, gazes at the horizon.

She sees the clouds that surround the dead,
the stolen guitar – birds on its strings.[81]

She travels on the bus line
along the green line[82] and the blue line –
valley and shoreline side by side.

The city of Salamis opposite you
is searching for new hideouts.
Engomi[83] on the left is trapped in the heartless light.

---

80 Regina: Regina is the best known and most mysterious female heroine in the legends and traditions of Cyprus. Found everywhere on the island, she is associated with ancient and medieval buildings, with beautiful locations, caves and ruins, springs and rivers, churches and chapels, plains and mountains, and fabulous hidden treasures. In the old legends she is associated with kings and warriors.

81 birds on its strings: On the road from Salamis to Trikomo, the electricity wires give the impression of the strings of a guitar.

82 Green line: The Green Line has existed since Christmas Day, 1963, when fighting between the Turkish and Greek communities of newly independent Cyprus resulted in the self-imposed partition of the city. The UK brokered a cease-fire between the two sides, and the Green Line, named after the green line drawn on a map by a British officer to show the division between the Greeks and Turks, came into being.

83 Engomi: With the collapse of the Mycenaean civilization there was Greek emigration from the Peloponnese after 1200 BC to Cyprus. Engomi was

Strength fills the oars.
Golden coins in the plaits of the waves
are dragged out to shore by Poseidon.[84]

A naked unwelcoming woman
with a thick flock of hair.
The Achaean saw her and desired her.

•

He sprang and tied her to his horse,
he bends over and kisses her. Cities, palaces,
arenas, theatres and market places sprout up.

This place is enchanted.
Time loses a tooth every now and then,
the wheel turns slowly and prudently.

With a rope, you can carry
a city on your back; you hang her
from a tree branch when you need to rest.

She can run away if she wants to, but she stays.
A naked woman who became the arch
over an aqueduct[85] – the water moves…

The news is bad; they've taken over the city
the next city and the one after that.
The children emerge from their hiding places.

January 1981

---

    established west of Famagusta, as the principal city and port; its massive city walls and houses of hewn stone indicate a high level of prosperity.

84   coins are … pushed to the shore by Poseidon: on the sands of Salamis many ancient coins were found, because a large part of the city is under the sea, maybe due to the earthquakes during the 4th century AD.

85   the arch over an aqueduct: an impressive Roman aqueduct to transfer water from the natural spring of Kefalovryso to Salamis. It was renovated by the Byzantines but destroyed during the Arab invasions (7th century AD).

BY AFFINITY

Half the city is in Larnaca
and the rest is in Limassol
with some remnants in Nicosia and Paphos,
making up the city I loved.

The limbs are scattered
in Abydos and Memphis,
in Elephantine, Thebes, Dendera, Heliopolis –
names of the deceased that hide
the God's limbs[86] in their soul.

Huge date-palms have sprung up at those places
(preparing the palm leaves)
and nomadic Jews with many flocks of sheep.
Birds have commenced their song
in the stream that God set aside
for irrigating the desert
not for cotton, but now for wheat,
generously bestowing on us
Demeter's best plaits.

They say that, behind the mountain,
from within the tunnel where we see the back of its voice,
that seed will fall here and there because it's a Greek seed.
And it will sprout and grow as I have foresaid.
And it will be dispersed in the river
that brings the crop as a body to the recipient.

---
86   "God's limbs": the limbs of God Osiris.

A bird deflowers with its beak
the unblemished shoreline
with a defiant mountain in the distance.

I have never seen such a big hole in the heart;
sunken ships loaded with looted treasures.[87]

There, they cast a copper query.

A woman pregnant with minerals[88]
gives birth to copper weapons, and removes the pigeons[89]
from the armpits of the great goddess.
With these, she breaks the resolve of Zeus,[90]
she wins the game with bloodless sacrifices
at a time when others reveal the man-goat,[91]
the crimson rain that falls on her sacrificial altar.

November 1980/January 1981

---

87   looted treasures: the Turkish invaders, plundered many goods from Cypriot houses in Kyreneia and Famagusta. They loaded the goods onto boats and shipped them off to Turkey.

88   pregnant with minerals: cf. Ovidius, *Metamorphoses*, X 531: "gravidamve Amathunta metallis", ie. Amathus is pregnant with metals. This area is rich in minerals, especially copper, since antiquity. cf. Plinius, *Naturalis Historia* and Theophrastus, *On Stones*.

89   pigeons: Sacred birds of Aphrodite. cf. Lucius Annaeus Cornutus, *Theologiae Graecae compendium*, 24 (199) and Nonnus of Panopolis, *Dionysiaca*, 33.178.

90   breaks the resolve of Zeus: cf. Sophocles, *Tragicorum,* Graecorum Fragmenta, Hildesheim, 1964, 855.15-17: Aphrodite conquers Zeus without a spear, without a javelin. Kypris Aphrodite shatters all the plans of mortals and immortals.

91   the man-goat: cf. Lactantius, *De falsa religione*, 1.21: "Apud Cyprios humanam hostiam Jovi Teucer immolavit". (In the country of Cypriots, Teucer sacrificed a carcass to Zeus.) See also Ovid: "hospes erat caesus! sacris offensa nefandis ipsa suas urbes Ophiusiaque arva parabat deserere alma Venus, 'sed quid loca grata, quid urbes peccavere meae? quod' dixit 'crimen in illis?" Ovid, *Metamorphoses,* X 228–231. ['Twas the blood of slaughtered guests! Outraged by these impious sacrifices, fostering Venus was preparing to desert her cities and her Ophiusian/Cypriot plains; 'but,' she said, 'wherein have these pleasant regions, wherein have my cities sinned? What crime is there in them?]

ABOLITION OF THE MOON

The ancestral moon
rising over the top of the hill
lies in wait for the enemy that goes to drink water.

It isn't really hiding
(who minds it, who is afraid of it?)
It isn't lactating, nor is it grazing.

Bright little moon that shines
through the darkness, to light the child's way.
He isn't going to school, to write in his books letters
that are scattered in empty heads.

One day I too caught it in the mud.
I had adopted Codrus'[92] rhythm.
I had stepped out for fresh air and to collect wood for the fire.
The good enemies of my grievous city
caught me out there and they save her.

On another occasion again, I changed
my name; I dubbed it "Cincinnatus".[93]
The myth of the Latin senator is well known:
"Hundreds and thousands of fellow country men

---

92 Codrus: the fabled last king of Athens (11th century BC). He sacrificed himself to save Athens from the invading Dorians.

93 Cincinnatus: Roman senator and army general (5th century BC), a patrician from the house of Quinctius), famous for his virtue and humility.

come running 'Run' they tell me,
'Duty calls; forget the oxen, march in the moonlight."
I had just finished my meal.

I put on my motherland,
took to the mountains,
I entered the city, they kneeled before me.
I depart together with a few daredevils.
I slay wild beasts – many miracles happen.
Then I return to my fields again.
What "motherland" means, I know not.
One of my goats died; what should I do?"

This is roughly what Cincinnatus said,
and the prow of the boat bent and kissed him.
The prow that was recording the actions
of his flock that belonged to his poor family.

Let no one falter or be afraid.
Wipe off the soil that is underfoot,
rid Peace of its sores
and caress our city as you should.

It wasn't his city; it is ours.
He wasn't a Greek; he was a Latin citizen.
He shouldn't have come along in the moonlight;
it's strange that he cares about us.

Codrus gave him a proper dressing down in the darkness:
"Whoever replicates our actions, is lost,
won over by Hades, forgotten forever.
Poor Cincinnatus …"
"Oh! Codrus, Codrus …"

January 1981

BODY OF CLAY

I am sorry to note, Famagusta,
that you are also responsible for what has become of us.
At a Public Assembly they offered you the crown
four times and you rejected it.

You then disappeared from our sight
so we can see you only in our dreams
and in the deception of sleep – yours and ours.

One day, God willing, when you awake
you will count the tops of our heads
and our disposed bottle-necks,
the froth of the sea, the drunken frogs
the desiccated snakes and a whole lot
of accidental compounds of silver, gold and steel.

With all these, the line of your senses will capture
a part of the world from all its regions.

All those born of you and me,
sacred cow-eyed wife of Zeus,
will glimpse the world through your vortex,
and they will also bear witness to this:

The crown you had rejected gazes upon
your heart with ruby eyes.

It splits your sleep in two, counting
the human figures on the shore.

The naked body emerging from the blue
roams on the softness of the sand.
It lies down and becomes a body of clay.

There and along the length of your coastline
the future (now the past) stirs.

Naked as you are, the birds bashfully see you
unimpeded embracing every passing conqueror,
drowning him in your monstrous kisses.

Slowly you sink, or rather you destroy yourself,
getting carried away by illusions.

The Providence of place and time
implore you, but you don't understand
to confess your great responsibility.

But I will force you with a pair of pincers.
What rotten teeth, what lost youth!
And yet I who had loved you once[94]…

August 1980, February 1981

---

94 And yet I who had loved you once: cf. Shakespeare, *Othello*, Act 5, Sc. 2 "Be thus when thou art dead and I will kill thee/And love thee after" and Othello's last words: "speak of one that loved not wisely, but too well".

THE DIFFERENCE

However strange it seems,
this city does not concern me at all:
(I know you somehow, I have met you somewhere).

You were beautiful in your youth. Your voice sounded
like a reed flute, while you braided your hair,
gazing at your silver reflection in the water.

An old story for children and Negroes.[95]
You and I, both, white under a damp sheet of mist,
on the verge of sorrow.

Roughly all of this was submitted to the squandering
of the mind, while a dead voice inside me roars.

Having plucked her feathers, the city was trapped
and left like a dead statue.

So that she would remember that the Resurrection
must not be preoccupied with manual labour.

She is a necessity, Where she is needed and When she is needed.

Squeezing past Pentadaktylos mountain
she apologises and she continues on foot.

---

95 Negroes: as a child, the poet used to read stories from Africa; he conceptualised the Negroes as the innocent children of humanity.

In a storage box she folds her wings
galvanised by the rising of the wind.

And I too "know you somehow."
And I won't be sorry to lose you once and for all.
What is the cost of a metope and a fulcrum?
Perhaps we will be a little lucky and it could cost nothing.

Do you hear me? Nothing. You don't concern me at all.

I close my eyes and I see you in another world,
where the sky blooms and the mountains are blessed.

Not you exactly; what can I do with you now?
The fullness of time fascinates me.

I knew the city once.
There I would shut the windows of my childhood,
and my eyes shed oil and wine[96]
that poured into vessels that I can't forget.

So, why, why should I remember you?
Why should I have met you, what was the need?
I know nothing, I am nothing
or if I think I am, I ask for forgiveness.

March 1981

---

96 oil and wine: Death – life. When oil is spilled, folklore has it as a bad omen. When wine is spilled it is seen as a good omen. On the roads of the "royal" graves of the necropolis of Salamis, huge amphorae full of oil and wine would accompany the dead.

AFTER MIDNIGHT

I don't know whether, having fallen,
Famagusta could be reborn at the end of the road
that is lit by fairy lights.

I have the pleasure to announce
that each of us offers our own solutions
according to the position of the moon and the sun.

Wanted! A city in good condition
with a garden and, if possible, a view towards the sea.
Please telephone during office hours and in the afternoon.

But the street vendor who had pre-sold
all the lottery tickets for the city, came crying
"what will become of my children and my wife,
I didn't know that I had children too,
and that my wife waits for me at home."
Crying he came, and he left crying even more.

Another also – a great athlete –
who had run nine thousand five hundred metres
and could hear the faint ringing at the finish line,
abandoned his race midway
"and I am not going anywhere, I want the city."

•

The race warden and the public objected but to no avail.
Πατρόκλυς άτλα.[97] What can I do? What can I do?
The general and the minister get angry.

Most Reverend and Honourable Representative,
parents of heroes, children of vagabonds.
Accept the shield of the multi-victorious athlete,
and the veils of the matrons[98] ... Quiet please!

March 1981

---

97 Πατρόκλυς άτλα: The Games of Patroclus. Inscription on a fragment from a jar (beginning of 6th century BC), made by the Attic potter and vase painter Sophilos.
98 the veils of the matrons: The famous veil of Laodice. She was the daughter of Agapenor (leader of the Arcadians in the Trojan War. Agapenor ended up in Cyprus after the war where he built the city of Paphos and the temple of Aphrodite). Laodice was known for having sent to Tegea a veil as a gift to Athena Alea and for having built a temple of Aphrodite Paphia in Tegea (Pausanias, 8. 53. 7).

SEIZURE OF A CITY

Wanting to catch the city as it was falling in my cot[99]
I faltered on Dante's harsh phrase "La materia é sorda".[100]
The mountain – thumb of the city –
wrapped in its dusty shawl,
was secretly provoking my childhood cunning.
I wouldn't be afraid,
if I didn't know that the world around me
is woven with senility and very beautiful injustice.
And I would be glad – my face shining like gold –
to receive its breath – like receiving life.

Lost in the stone-fight of the stars
spitting blood, while hauling the chariot
of the sun's daughter by its hair,
I hold back the deep darkness.

The day came and went, commenting,
flying calmly on the pigeon's breast.

Unclear things unfold in the place
where they happened in the past.
Time leans towards them, unadulterated.
The city registered in the telephone book

---

99   falling in my cot: "An artist is a person who believes in the existence of the perceivable world, like the child who wants to grab the sun ray as it shines into its cot" (Théophile Gautier). And: "I found myself in the innocent state of the child in its cot who believes that he can catch the bird flying in the sky" (René Magritte).

100 La materia é sorda: Matter is deaf (Dante).

contemplates a sea and handmade trees.
Buses of this route criss-cross the city
with the names of enslaved villages written overhead.

Ochre flows on the unimaginable and forgotten cheek
below the stone of the mountain.
Green, untidy grasses of the sky
on the beaks of two or three birds.

March 1981

MADONNA OF THE GOLDEN CAVE[101]

Every time a bomb fell on her head
she would turn and ask what was happening.
She knew the answer from when she was born
but she could not believe it.

Being a woman, with a sad face,
hidden beneath a silk apron,
she smells the lilies like the other
Madonna Della Cava of Lower Famagusta.[102]

The latter woman was unlucky; with God's will,
she sighs under the yoke of slavery.
While the former, God bless her, awaits
the hand that will lift her apron.

The cow-eyed and humble Virgin
holds her Son in her arms in by-gone times.
Time is a void, she sees it,
and her gaze suffices to announce it.

---

101 Madonna of the Golden Cave: a Greek church dedicated to Jesus' Mother Mary; it is carved on the side of a limestone hill, close to the airport, at Deftera village. It was bombed by the Turkish air force in 1974.

102 Lower Famagusta: George Jeffery, *A Description of the Historic Monuments of Cyprus*, Nicosia, 1918, p. 225, "In Famagusta, there is pagan tomb carved on the side of a stone … During the middle-ages this underground temple was known in the lingua-franca of the Mediterranean, as the Madonna Della Cava." cf. also, a description by Nicholas de Martoni, Peregrinatio (1394 AD).

She refreshes her soul and my spirit
from a bucket that she uses to wash her hair
in the hole of a boulder under the sea monster's light.
Her robe flutters with a secret smile.

•

I am going to sleep, help me Madonna
to rest my body and soul.
Help refine my mind
as it no longer has any hope at all.

Voice: "You will return." Even if we do return
do you think it will be the city that we left behind?
An example I believe will convince you;
when the years pass and you return
to a person you had once loved –
to a person you had once loved –
my God, how much times change!

I tell you this, Madonna of the Golden Cave, and tuck it
in securely in your head scarf;
hope is a deep sorrow and nothing more;
of someone who sinks sloppily
in the sand of an empty sky, someone who descends
with all his original charms, to applaud you.

Hush now, so we can look at this bomb
that's falling on both of our heads.
On my part, I save the word
in this hideout close to a shattered aerodrome.

Is it not a coincidence that in those days
wearing an army helmet,[103] chanting the hymn

---

103 wearing a helmet: the poet worked as a broadcaster during the invasion. He was making rousing speeches to strengthen people's spirits. For security, he had to wear an army helmet.

of freedom to the trees and the rivers,[104]
while collecting beautiful pebbles and branches
for my own son, a seven-year-old at the time,
I was looking up to you for support, oh Blessed one?[105]

The war would end one day, we all knew it,
we would be mourning at the houses of the dead
the lengthy journey ... That's gone too.

But you and I, buried so many years
in the illusion of things that can be resurrected,
we used to call the place a void – a void forever.

March 1981

---

104 collecting pebbles and branches: During the broadcasts, we'd have a break; the miracle of life was asking for its own rights.

105 Oh Blessed one: "Cyprus, quae olim (Macaria) id est beata inaula est in sinu Carpathii maris sita" (Claudio Duchetti, 1570); "Cyprus was blissful once and now is blessed, an island that lies in the Carpathian Sea."

RESURRECTION HYMN

Let's overlook everything that harms
the heart, stomach, chest and kidneys.

Let's suppose that wolves and foxes
have banished themselves; death is simplified.

The chickens roam free on the road,
the sheep regulate the traffic.

The ants free of duties and ignored
are digging a tower to receive the gifts.

A melon seed, straw, a kernel,
a fly thrown on the side of a ditch.

A swarm of people is leaving.
One to build a nest, sixth floor,
another to throw a fishing line to the sky.

You are in the middle of the infuriated city-square
smashing plates (that appear like a curved trajectory).[106]

The target quivers every time you hit it.
It promises to reciprocate the visit.

•

And it arrives as you knew it would;
such is the city-square, the porcelain and the gaze.

---

106 a curved trajectory: cf. the trajectory of mortars.

A gnashing of teeth is heard and wastage.
In large clinics a river of blood is being shed
sweeping along swollen corpses of sheep,
bicycle wheels, garments, shoes.

A loud tumult where the lance falls.
You rise covered in plaster
and run to scare the darkness.

Behind you, are thousands of candles.
I can't single out hands and balloons;
the never-fading light follows you to the grave.
You dismount to take a breath.

This is what the Creator saw with his own eyes
and He was smiling until the next day.
He took the eraser and a pencil
and He, the Judge, called the holy witnesses.

Here, he told them, was Greece,
at the far end; Cyprus, further south; Egypt.
Higher up; Turks, and further north; Russians.
Here are the lakes, their shadows can be seen.

You know what you should do; tell
all the nations that I command
the delivery of the city that was pulled apart,
it's re-assembly and collection.

And before the others had time to react, He signed it.

April 1981

EFFIGY

Now that shipwrecked sails can be seen on the ocean,
the sea, as if enchanted, is motionless.

The city is left bitter and limping
with its wild horns raised.

Three old men[107] were tied together, while you stirred,
and called out to her "Constantia,[108] my daughter!"

The city grinned at you with respectful hatred;
she had many things to do for you later on.

She throws down children heavy like statues –
they lie on your striped apron.

Svelte antics of terracotta,
a nest that is felled by a wretched wind
carried on the wings of a swallow.

---

107 Three old men: The old men of the Sea: Phorcys, Nereus and Proteus. Also, Leo Tolstoy's "Three Hermits": "The three old men, hand-in-hand were running upon the water."

108 Constantia, my daughter: in 350 AD, Emperor Constantine II, rebuilt Salamis that had been destroyed by an earthquake (345 AD) and named it Constantia. (In Latin it means steadfast). In 648 AD, with the Arab invasions, Constantia was destroyed and its inhabitants moved five kilometres south, to a village considered to be the remains of Arsinoe, a city built in 274 BC by Ptolemy Philadelphus in honour of his sister. Gradually this settlement evolved to become the city of Famagusta.

A smile that you received in your bosom
with fire flies swallowing it,
birds picking at it with their beaks.

The shrew-city in a hovel
is indicated by your right hand.

∙

Don't dream, don't hope,
be the lover of pain.

In those harsh years,[109] those frugal years,
even angels loathed one another.

Shrunken to a sunken island
oh my city, oh my island, oh my foothold, why?

After this I wouldn't have anything more to add,
except for removing the veil.

May 1981

---

109 those harsh years: meaning the years after the death of President Makarios (1977).

FOR THE CITY WHICH VOTED FOR THOSE WHO BROUGHT HER TO THIS POINT

I considered you wiser, at the upper echelon.
I believed you to be mother superior; what do I see now?

I would not dare to search for you even in my dreams,
since you have now become Cyprus the shape of a snake.

If I knew who you were voting for,[110] I would not
have taken you down from the iconostasis,[111]
I would refuse nourishment to my heart,
I would not throw bran to my chickens.

Now it's too late and you must die.[112]
Lady, I regret, there is no time
even for a prayer[113] and you must die.

---

110 voting for: the parliamentary elections of 24 May 1981.
111 iconostasis: the most prominent feature of an Orthodox church is the iconostasis, consisting of one or more rows of Icons and religious paintings. It itself symbolises the world of saints and angels – the Heavenly Kingdom, to us not yet fully attainable.
112 you must die: cf. Shakespeare, *Othello*, Act 5, Sc. 2.
113 no time even for a prayer: *Othello*, Act 5, Sc. 2.

She was startled in her sleep.
She put the fear of angels in him too,
running around the city walls in her impressive attire –
that she had inherited from her mother[114] (that is not sufficient)
it was a bad dream[115] –
the hands reach for the pillow –
there's Iago with the vote,
he drops it through the keyhole –
not under the wide door – the fake one –
like a love letter,
and this black man, burnt even more than coal
and widowed by his own two hands
in the end, he kisses again and again[116]
the utopia of his youth, and wipes it.

May 1981

---

114 she inherited it from her mother: *Othello*, Act 3, Sc. 4, "An Egyptian woman gave the handkerchief to my mother … She told her, while she kept it 'twould make her amiable and subdue my father entirely to her love."

115 it was a bad dream: *Othello*, Act 5, Sc. 2, "Oh, this is unbearable! Oh, the horror! There should be a huge eclipse of the sun and the moon …"

116 he kisses again and again: cf. *Othello*, Act 5, Sc. 2.

THE STRANGE DREAM[117]

I am seeing a strange and peculiar mystery.[118]

A Fury appeared in my sleep
to see what I was doing. I was asleep, of course.
I was playing with a big wooden animal,
I think I was tickling its dewlap
on a bridge, that was wooden too,
while behind me my principal was asking
– this is good too! – if *galoshes*
should be spelt with an "a" or a "u".
But who has time for such quibbles;
linguistics, contingents of death...
But let it be, for his sake, a dictionary
(by Zikides) has nothing on the question.

It was then that the Fury lost it for good,
her liver swelled out of all proportions,
beating herself, and asking why, why, why, why?

It was a mission sent wrongly to the city-square:
She found poor me, on whom
to weave her web, and I would break it,
and then she would persecute me as if I were Orestes,[119]

---

117 Title: cf. *The Iliad*, 2: 56, 'θεῖος ὄνειρος' (sacred dream).
118 Inscription: cf. Kosmas Aetolos, *Song of Dawn at Christmas*
119 *Orestes*: Greek tragedy by Euripides (408 BC).

while I become Rimako[120] and she would lose me.
And she would find again the beginning of her thread
from the gap – the chimney – of the dream,
while dropping a bunch of fresh hopes,
and I would tear her apart, torturing
her in thousands of places producing blisters
on the surface of her body, oh, what a life!

– "Who is this Fury?"
A faithful friend asks me with a smile.

I had woken up. Familiar shores;
slippers and books, the chirping of birds.

– We shall see further along, we shall find
the answer following the course of the poem.
The poem knows. It takes shape slowly,
like the painting of a child.
At the end, we shall find out.
Forbearance, patience and faith are needed.

Sleep, full of peculiar dreams
that are lost in the abyss of another dream
or an awakening created at the peak
of an ancient sleep elevated to the breast of a careless Fury
who chases after an illusion and is demeaned.

Let's not exaggerate and get carried away by that
which we imagine to be spread out in front of our eyes.

The Fury exists as an amalgam
of the girl who slipped out from the House

---

120   Rimako: a persona that objectifies the emotions of the poet.

of her feared Father. Let's say it's like this:
She opened the door and went out.

And while leaving, she met the dove of the soul,
better at the climax of its sleep,
and she took a piece from her too.

Once she used to be a daughter of Justice.[121]
She was like her ideal lady of the castle.
Now encircled by snakes and wild beasts
she can't breathe, she asks me for affection.
How can I help her? Was it my fault she wasn't born?
That she attempts to pass through the other door
of light which is still being created
and is not formed until the morning of the next Day?

Very complex miracles – What can I do?
Was it God's will for us to live
with Kyrenia like a wedge in our eyes
and Famagusta, – the harlot Famagusta –
becoming like the pool of Siloam?
And what's with this? Who defines the truth,
what is a lie, and what are the weighing scales?

Since you don't come from our parts
foreigner, think about Alexander's journey.
The Macedonian phalanx,
Babylon, the Indus River, the total glory
and the methods of the earth's tribes.
Ocean, if you are not created from this foreigner's
body, take from him too,

---

121 a daughter of Justice: Guardian of the laws. cf. Heraclitus, "The Sun shall not surpass the defined standards, otherwise the Furies, who are servers of Justice, will discover him." (Diels-Kranz, *Die Fragmente der Vorsokratiker*, Berlin, 1960, p. 94.)

Osiris, Buddha, Zeus, King of Kings.
Jesus Christ Victorious. And now drink.

May 1981

MARCH TOWARDS FAMAGUSTA

Through the broken glass of time
the hand of God emerged
with the unerring eye
and the bicycle wheel
around His head – immortal demon!

Having sobered from His wilful stupidity
he takes counter measures
against the masquerading
of the earthly sphere.

And there's the Virgin,
his daughter from Anna,
in her hand she weighs up
his looks and shadow.

These memories
that now hang
over our heads
could become good carrier pigeons
or the poking of the fire
which we will reignite.

A huge water-temple
will gnaw at its carcass

invoking
the terrorist feast.

The statue of Saint Mammon
supervised by Moloch
cries out saying "my children."

We hope these few examples
together with the pictures
provide an idea
of the pending morrow.

Eat, drink; because tomorrow
the limpet-eaters
will deprive you of your souls.

The city, now in the unclaimed merchandise of Leontiadis,[122]
will remain buried there by Zeus
who has not honoured her even with one lightning bolt!

Beneath old discarded objects
and the butchered couches
with their white straw bodies,
that are so poor for pity and for sale.

The city, a forgotten whore,
with blood stained lips
and eyes painted blue
with a red hue.

And from the centre
of your brave light-beam,
you look at the cross-eyed hand

---

122 Leontiadis: very well-known trader of second hand items in Famagusta.

of a pasteurised god, and
you dress your lover
in satin and in lots of gold.

And now I, a dwarf of some repute,
in a pitiful state,
I roam the market place in my tunic and sandals.

The theatre curtain brushes over my face;
and from the wings, a stage hand
takes my cross.

Though I am free to depart or die
I decide to await my arrival.

May 1981

THE STORY OF
THE CIVIL GUARD

One time my birth place
took to her heels
(the soldiers' tactical withdrawal[123] had preceded this
– not a single one of them remained as an example,
not even fifty determined lepers).
And the conqueror camped
around the city. He couldn't believe
that the "banquet" was left for him untouched
(everyone had left, even cats and mice –
and no one contemplated tying down even with a piece of string
anything insecure).[124]
Within three days he cautiously entered the city.

Here I note the story of the civil guard Andreas, the grocer.[125] Since he was my parents' neighbour, I called him on the telephone[126] on the third day of being surrounded. I was not expecting anyone to answer the call – I tried my luck, because when you are already lost, desperate, you hope for anything. He answered but he didn't say the customary

---

123 tactical withdrawal: the radio broadcasts of the Cyprus National Guard made the following stereotypical announcement during the Turkish invasion: "Our army is falling back smoothly."

124 anything insecure: there was no attempt at sabotage to at least delay the attack of the Turks as they found the city ready for the taking.

125 Andreas, the grocer: Andreas Tymbios; who had a small grocery shop in Hilarion Street.

126 Telephone: his number was 031-62454.

"You called the wrong number, we don't have a telephone," but instead "Your parents left with the others. Only very few of us civil guards remain. The Turks haven't put in an appearance, what do you say now? We are going to the market for perishables. I take some for me, that is. Who can I sell them to?" This could have been the last phone call made in the city before it was taken over.

Continuation of the story: when the Turks entered the city for good, Andreas took refuge in the house of a bed-ridden old lady, whose children did not have enough time to take her along with their luggage. We don't know if the lady symbolised the city, time will tell. "Don't be sad mother," Andreas used to say to her. Now you have me as your child. I am also being hunted, determined to survive by stealing food for both of us in the evenings from my shop. Even if I wanted to run away, I couldn't any longer. We are surrounded by Turkish violets and in the centre there's you and me.

Days and long nights passed. Searching, the Turks approached the old lady. Hidden, Andreas came out to the open fields suffering, disappearing into the darkness, setting off the dogs' barking and volleys. Thanks to his beard that was intermingling with grass and his arms that looked like dried tree branches, he managed to slip away around a bend. He arrives at the first hill of the Pan-Hellenes, asks, learns, runs and finds his wife in a refugee settlement. He enters the tent and finds her asleep. He lies down beside her, worn out by exhaustion. His three daughters, his three Fates were fast asleep. At some stage his wife is startled awake by a bad dream. She sees a stranger next to her and screams. Who is this man wanting to dishonour me? She takes a plank and hits him. The daughters wake up. Many people, children and lots of dust gather around. He kneels. I am your husband. I am Andreas of Hilarion Street. Grocer by profession. No, I am not dead. She kisses him and covers him with the blanket. Tears rain upon his dried whiskers. His daughters anoint him with incense.

Children sprinkle rose-leaves and rice over him. A priest chants over him "Those who God ..."

> End of the story and return
> to the second and distressing time: A country in exile
> votes for those who shackled it to slavery.
>
> Memory has no children,[127] she is a sterile woman.
> The man of virtue, the lover of art
> contemplates only what he sees.

Opening a parenthesis, we also say this: We know that when we return all this will be as useful as an old rhythm. Someone must talk about all this. A great benefactor – a donor must save this. Later, we will rely on it to create history. Because from here, there will be a new beginning. A monument will then be erected, dedicated to all that was lost throughout the valley. A solid monument of copper and concrete – to adorn this city.'

May 1981

---

127 Memory has no children: cf. from the poem *Lyre* by Andreas Kalvos.

ARDANA[128]

He could see half of his yard with his eyes closed
from a place where, at other times,
not even a stone could be seen.

The miracle was in the dream, but even that was half.
Because while he was standing under the grape vine
of a good neighbour looking towards the yard
of his beloved home, how could he proceed,
as some foreigners had set up a feast with dancing in the open.

And all of them were looking at him,
raising their chins towards the sky
continuously signalling "no."

At another time, he succeeded
in entering his home through a crack in his dream.
Coming into the yard from the arch
he found the Turkish woman drawing water.

He didn't even think to ask her why.
He only took his familiar towel –

---

128 Ardana: a village on the mountain ranges of Pentadaktylos, eighteen miles from Famagusta. The idea of the poem came after the National Theatre Director, Andreas Marangos told me one day: "You write about Famagusta, which one day may be given back. But who would think about my village Ardana? I think it will never be given back. I know it even from my dreams. I think we have lost it forever." The poet thought that Famagusta was in the more tragic position. It was our city and we let it slip through our hands. Now we see her and then we don't see her. Will we ever live again in our city?

the light blue one – and wiped his face.
She turned quietly, without a word
and motioned somewhat (movement of the hands)
as if she was saying "It's not our fault,
it's what we found, and we haven't touched anything.
What can I do? If you wish, join us for a meal."

The man who went into his yard
said to the poet: Kyriako, all this means that
we will never return to our village.
Yes, it is tragic, but better to know it
than to live in the darkness of a different hope.
In my dream, I approached my home many times
and in my dream I found
the way to break through the line – I flew there,
I saw it as I could not see it
even during peaceful and measured times.

But he continued saying that some people were preventing him
from entering, they were dissuading him: "As soon as I approached
they would not let me proceed.
And I could not even leave again.
There was no exit in my dream
and I had no alternative but to wake up."

The poet listened to him attentively
and he smiled with measured words.
"Though we let Famagusta slip through our hands," he said,
"one day we will certainly retake it
but under humiliating terms; that's the truth."

Know this only: Either you see her
and you can't retake her directly

or you can't see her and you are under the illusion
that you see her, because that's how it seems.
This is the worst part. Look, it's as if
the guards are there preventing you
from entering the tunnels of memory,
you'd think they prohibit passage
even to the flight of the mind.
However, your poor village of Ardana, let's make it tipsy,
on the slope of Pentadaktylos mountain,
Sir Toby,[129] with wine from Illyria.
Let's drink to its health, as long as
Atlas holds up the Universe on his shoulders.
Because time passes and nature is being lost.
The sea that is now melting into silk
come tomorrow will turn into a beast, beware!
At that time I may go mad
and you may re-enter your own home.

June 1981

---

129 Sir Toby: Shakespeare's hero in *The Twelfth Night*; the play takes place in Illyria. Toby is a wine lover, and heavy drinker but a benevolent character.

WINGED SUN

And the sun says, "There she is over there"
implying that we are approaching
her land, her sea.
Naturally we can see her from the bulwark of the ship
as we fly eastwards.
With a few petrified sheep on the edge
and trees with dead branches... Truth
is not found in what you see; don't believe
in miracles and their bitter slaughter.
The world is full;
with moments of happiness here and there
when you forget yourself, immortal one.

So, hide the ink of sorrow
deep inside you and if you have any left over, give
some to this poor man – me.
I want to write how much you loved her
under the shade of a pine tree, next to a boulder.
Because, if the sun that points her out saying "there she is"
could see her better, it would discern you
as a small ant on her body,
on the edge of her hand, on the cleavage
of her breast promenading her with
a melon seed between clenched teeth.

But you too, would have seen it from up high.

July 1981

THE WIND GOD

I adore imagination.
Seeing you and imagining that I don't see you
fascinates me most.

But I believe that you too, accept me without realizing it.
Hold on to your freshness, my girl,
and I shall drag the sea with a turtle...

The man who'd descend forty feet below
and would hang his voice in the darkness
(stone of darkness – digging in the darkness
with the nails of his song –
digging the stone in his darkness)
the pitman was singing at high noon.

How beautiful is man,
sweet is the star that covers him
day and night in cold and in rain
who laughs and howls at the sun.

And then sunset. Sunset of Cyprus, you are
lovely and long lasting.

The sun is not afraid of the smoke;
a bird crosses over it, a mountain half-hides it.

The painter's words return:
"If you paint a tree over the moon, it will have one."

Fine, then. And now what will he say
about you, sun, as you recline in all seriousness
on the red lawn of the sky
and he doesn't dare to look at you? – I think.

Pouring a little tea towards the places
of the one who owned land, but had
not a drop of water to water it with,
he measures the earth that will collect us all.

And then, the immortal city, although tired,
will fall into a swoon – a monster of the lake;
that will suddenly reappear to allay
silence, and engender a bitter little almond tree.

Everything exists; both those lost and those present.
Everything is blown away by the wind God.

August 1980

THE WAVES

And Rimako said to his city:
– "We had a good time last night."
– "I think so," she replies, "it wasn't bad."
I mean to say, good... Very good!
– "Wonderful," she again replied. That suffices for me.
To look at you four miles away
and to imprint your image in my mind.
– People don't understand your words my Lord,
and neither do I. (She smiles.)
"In a meadow where the light is everlasting ..." (Pause.) And:
– What do you know of me? Who am I?
– You are the city that has become a pigsty[130]
from within the city walls to the scattered stones.
Sixty-five and three hundred churches[131]
have sprouted in your pastures ...

One day, when I was little, I too was skipping in the fields and I found myself deep within you. An animal was howling at the edge (at other times the Holy Altar). I was afraid, and I raised my eyes. And I saw a saint – the last one – the poor piece from a wall fresco, tearfully gazing at me.

---

130 pigsty: with the Ottoman invasion of Cyprus in 1571 AD, the Christian churches of Famagusta were turned into storerooms and stables. cf. Agnes Michaelides, *The Old Famagusta*, Nicosia, 1970.

131 sixty-five and three hundred churches: according to oral tradition, in the past, they built 365 churches in Famagusta so that one church would have a liturgy for each day of the year.

Rimako, I hope you are not still looking at me. There is no more worship of love, there is no reason for you to sing. It was a mistake to think that I was drawn to the midnight blade of your light. Perhaps I was deceived by the waves and believed in all that was a lie. Perhaps I was confused by the fire emanating from the burning stumps. But now...

– Madam, I will stop talking and crying ... The withered words and tears ... Hidden thoughts... Goodbye and farewell.

– Farewell Pylades,[132] my friend. Don't forget to pass on my greeting to Orestes.

– I will take both them and the perfume bottle.

September 1981

---

132 Pylades: friend of Orestes in the tragedy of Euripides, *Iphigenia in Tauris* (413 BC).

TYMPANI OF LOVE

> *... and then you will conclude, I think, that, if*
> *according to Eustathius, the island Cyprus resembles the*
> *skin of a sheep, the condition of the island is*
> *the fleeced body of this animal decaying*
> *from wounds, worms and various insects.*
> G. S. Menardos[133]

"The love, oh, the love for my city is
a diabolical task. It has no beginning and no end.
It enters through the branches
of the calm waves, it pours into
sluggish, dark words,
it chooses according to its judgement."

Such are the words spoken by the locust with incurable threads
and with a dye of independent[134] knowledge
it keeps saying that love and love...

Until a leper wrapped in clean poplin gauze
arrives to falsely testify about adultery.

Under cross-examination he states he doesn't mean
the soft raisins and the songbirds,
the rich carobs and other fortifications.

---

133 G. S. Menardos: Vice-Council of Greece stationed in Cyprus (1869) during the last years of the Ottoman occupation.
134 independent knowledge: the Christian Church of Cyprus is Autocephalous. This privilege was granted by the Byzantine Emperor Zenon, in 488 AD, to the Bishop Anthemios of Constantia (later Famagusta).

Whilst, you, oh love, tearfully gaze upon him
dying with you, and you keep him warm.
You are a perfect woman like the desert,
smooth and soft, full of breasts
that bounce in the freshly shaven wind.
At times you shrink and at times you grow
according to the beast you have in mind.
Sometimes you bark strangely, and those
who have heard you howling in pain,
say that's how your beads sound too.

It's better then, with the locust
and the fairy tales of the lepers.
Better that I feel that you exist
behind the mountain and down by the bush.

If Cyprus resembles a sheep's skin,
the fleeced body is decaying
with wounds, full of worms and the horror of insects.

Why shouldn't I too forget you
muffled in the bushes of the rocky terrain?
Not wanting to hear, to see, or feel warm.

I fear love that destroys time
and with one grasp, renders the clock useless.
That which senses the bitter cup of sorrow
and loneliness, gnawing at the flesh.
This is the love I fear and no-one else.
This is why I won't call love, love.

September 1981

BATON

And who, my little girl, made you a Turk?
Who did such a terrible thing to you?
Had you no parents? Didn't they look for you?
Had you no relative to trace your whereabouts?
　　　　　　　　　　　　Vasilis Michaelides[135]

They tied the city to the bell tower
with chains made from the bodies of brave young men
and some remains of statues.

The message that the city had been conquered
for the umpteenth time was brought by a Turk[136]
after he got it from a Greek traitor[137]
who got it from an Englishman[138] and the Englishman from a Turk[139]
and he, from a Venetian,[140] a Frank[141] and a Templar[142]
and from knights and monks paid by the British

135　Vasilis Michaelides: cf. his poem *The Woman of Chios*, 1821. The woman was abducted by the Turks from the island of Chios in 1821 and sold to an Ottoman chief in Cyprus.
136　brought by a Turk: Turkish invasion of Cyprus, 20 July 1974.
137　a Greek traitor: the Greek Junta staged a military coup in Cyprus, 15 July 1974.
138　an Englishman: Cyprus was an English colony, 1878–1960.
139　a Turk: Cyprus was under Ottoman occupation, 1571–1878.
140　a Venetian: Cyprus was under Venetian occupation, 1489–1571.
141　a Frank: Cyprus was under the Franks, 1191–1489.
142　Templar: The Catholic Military Order of the Templars bought Cyprus from Richard the Lionheart for 100.000 Byzantine coins. To avoid resistance from the people of Cyprus, the Templars sold Cyprus to Guy De Lusignan (1191) and they got their money back.

midway on the high seas en route to liberate
the Holy Lands; Crusaders and Lionhearts –
great is their name; saved the land
from the clutches of the Byzantines and the Arabs[143]
who had made the baton a black horse
and a yellow ship – the Romans[144] are to blame too
club wielders with the cat-o'-nine-tails of love
for ancient arenas and wine drinking
in front of the furthest shrine of the Ptolemies.[145]
And what were they aiming to do
to a great island with ten kingdoms[146]
that were paying a tribute tax to the Persians[147]...
I suggest we exempt the dwellers of Salamis and Evagoras[148] for a while;
he kept the Greek culture going in his homeland
simply because he had the power –
a blend of an Athenian tyrant and a lover of the arts.

Now then, the Persians and later the Egyptians[149]
– with the baton this time of pure ivory –

---

143 Byzantines and Arabs: Cyprus was a state of the Byzantine Empire (330–1191 AD). The Arab invasions of Cyprus started in the seventh century and lasted until the tenth century.

144 the Romans: Roman occupation of Cyprus (58 BC–330 AD).

145 Ptolemies: the Ptolemies ruled Cyprus from 294 BC to 58 AD.

146 Ten Kingdoms: the ancient kingdoms of Cyprus had a Mycenaean origin.

147 paying a tribute tax to the Persians: Before the Persian occupation of Cyprus (480–449 BC) the Cypriot Kings had to pay a subjugation fee to the Great King of Persia, since the 6th century, in order to retain their political independence.

148 Evagoras: the most important political figure of ancient Cyprus. He ascended to the throne of Salamis (411 BC) by overthrowing the Phoenician embezzlers. He cultivated the Greek civilisation by inviting philosophers and artists from Greece. His vision was to unite the kingdoms of Cyprus and escape from the hegemony of the Persians. His resistance lasted from 391 to 380 BC. The Persians dominated in the end. His political opponents assassinated Evagoras and his son Pnytagoras in 374 BC.

149 Egyptians: the Pharaoh Amasis II (569–525 BC) forced the Cypriots to pay him a subjugation fee.

and then the Assyrians[150] and some of the Phoenicians
then Greeks again, right at the beginning, like the great Mycenaeans[151]
with their gleaming helmets and their plumes
over their visor-covered heads
and their shields first and best of all,
with a baton from an acquired spear
watching and supporting them.

Time to go back to the bodies of young heroes
who adorned their life
with a glorious death like that of the three hundred Spartans.[152]

The city was asleep in her dream
precious and alone,
dissipating every associated evil
felt that tomorrow would be better.
She wakes and sees black death before her.
She untangled herself from the net, and ran to forestall them
from taking her immortal head –
too late though! Her hands blocked the flowing blood.

Bare, with light falling on her knee-pad
and fingers painted with henna.

Joyous, the Grim Reaper tripped on the body
whispering amorous words of blood to it.
He took up all its joys and plucked them.

---

150 Assyrians: 8th/7th century BC. An inscription on a stele in the Berlin Museum reports that seven Cypriot Kings were paying a subjugation fee to the Assyrian King Sargon II (709 BC).

151 Mycenaeans: Mycenaean merchants settled in Cyprus after the end of the 15th century BC until the 12th century BC, with the mythical arrival of the heroes of the Trojan War who established the Cypriot kingdoms.

152 three hundred Spartans: the 300 Spartans with their leader Leonidas who died defending Greece from the Persians in the Battle of Thermopylae (480 BC).

He dismantled all the doors and windows.[153]

Let them think of the Famagustians as cowards;
they were Famagusta's gold and ivory offspring.
All of those who are scattered everywhere,
do not refute the prosperous, who,
reaping riches from their hard work,
found a common fate in wastefulness,
in the supermarket[154] of refugees.

I am referring to the inhabitants who did not possess
the resilience to fill the city
with a raging presence, with faith and tenacity.
And they hurriedly evacuated the city
in the time it takes for the sound of a plane.
They scattered all over in the orchards
till the danger had passed, they dug mass
graves for themselves. The baton
of the Turks had reached above their heads
and it forced them to live once and for ever
like the un-tuned guitar with a broken string.

As for you, Famagusta, what can I say to you?
You had an army and a police force
and courts and bunkers.

You had wireless, army vehicles, trenches
and army officers tested
in the battles of 1946 to '49.[155]

---

153 he dismantled all the doors and windows: after the invasion the Turks dismantled the houses of Famagusta.

154 in the supermarket of refugees: after the invasion some refugees tried to continue enjoying life's good times. For example, in the refugee settlement of Strovolos, in the first crucial months, there was a sign: "Bingo every Friday: Prize a gold coin."

155 the battles of 1946 to '49: during these years there was a civil war in Greece; some of

And all of them scampered off
taking with them their binoculars and their compasses.

The new relay runners found you then,
defenceless, without land mines.
On the outskirts of Lower Famagusta
and in the sweet scented orchards of Saint Memnon —
"Remember the city," the sign said to them:
"Welcome to the city of the orange tree."

Your inhabitants were terrified
and the city was taken like spilled water.
Before your sweet scent, now rises the victor
holding the horn of Selene.[156]

"It's all yours, Turks, taken with your blood,
that is, with the sweat of your blood,"[157]
howled the hawkish bold man,
honorary citizen and recipient of the key to the city.

He blocks the city's entry with barrels.[158]

War that achieves its primary goal.

The tanks grazed in the meadow
(their excrement was putrid,
their words burn on your face)
as they tried to saddle the land.

---

the Army Officers who were stationed in Cyprus had participated in that civil war.
156 a horn of Selene: the sickle of Hades, a half-moon; on 14 August 1974, Famagusta was taken by the Turks; (eve of the Assumption of Mary); the moon was in its 26th day.
157 the sweat of your blood: see footnote 30.
158 He blocks the city's entry with barrels: the barrels were placed by the Turkish occupation forces; photos of the city present such a view.

Children are running and playing with their fear.

The city is surrounded with spikes
twisted rope around its horns
with a bell hanging from her neck.

When she grows up they will slaughter her.

Almost with reverence they grab her.
Lips of the city that were kissing their weapons.
The law will release its odour:
"Welcome to the city of the orange tree."
And the city can't escape its nature
otherwise the orange tree will die.

The city has covered her thin blood
with familiar worship of heart and wine.

She stands complete in the middle eye of the sun.

The light does not disengage from its spot
except for the shadow at every move.

And as much as you wanted to call her the pearlescent city
you wouldn't fall far out of its walls, I think.

This is not automatic, it has a prehistory.
It needs emotion, a pull on the trigger
and hearing impaired fig leaves.

Rejoice, Turks, as children rejoice for a great gift;
a city, of high stature, with all its dowry,
pleads with you "take me and empty me,
fill your boats with unique and divine things,

may your deceased be forgiven."

They enter and what do they find!
A city adorned with the veil of torture.
Well prepared for the constriction, the restriction
the brilliant resilience.

Oh, cheerful orange tree![159] Arrange
for the city to be stabbed in its cradle
before she could utter the word "mother".[160]

With little knowledge we arrive at the shoreline
which disembarks the Turks before Othello.[161]

They will take half the city from the city.
(They stabbed her female belly with a bayonet.)

At the sight of their tanks a diffidence.

Your sword-like eyes would have repelled them.

The thunderous voices of the orange trees
were trampling the shadow of death.

From the conch of your north-western ear
when sleep was sticking to the foliage

"We shall live together 'les Grecs and Turks',

---

159 Oh, cheerful orange tree: cf. poem by Angelo Vlahos, *The land of Greece*: Do you the land where/ the cheerful orange tree blooms/ the vine tree reddens/ the olive tree blossoms/ Oh, it is known by all/ it is the Hellenic land."
160 utter the word mother: "Land of old gods and new demigods" (Angelo Vlahos); he also taught us to pronounce the words "military coup."
161 Othello: Shakespeare's play *Othello* is set in Venice and Famagusta Castle in Cyprus. The bastion of the castle facing the sea is associated, in the people's imagination, to Othello.

we don't have any more death to give
as we have spent it all."

That's how the wooden hope measures
the people in the museum of statues.
Those who do not understand history
and do not redeem geography.

A crowd of defenceless martyrs
from within the rocks and torrents.
A soul with so many flowers around the line of the face
blossoms sweetly on its mountains and their windows.

September 1980/October 1981

FREE-FIELD STYLE VASE

*And the wings of the future
darken the past, the beak and
claws have desecrated History.*
                              T. S. Eliot

A bird with a broken spark on its head
arrived at the shallows of Famagusta.

Fifteen years had passed
since receiving the last kiss from its parents
who then died in foreign lands.
And they had placed a red ring,[162]
a sacred bond, so that it wouldn't forget to look fully upon
the city of its forefathers.

They made it vow to go to an old
school ground[163] (with arches and such like)
which housed free-field style vases.

"There you will see your beloved ones,
your famous wife and your children,
just before they were lost without rhyme or reason in a lake.

You will also see your grandfather's picture,

---

162 a red ring: migratory birds with a marker, subjects to scientific research.
163 old school ground: The old Girls' Primary School became the Municipal Museum of Famagusta.

a spitting image of you, if we add the fish[164]
that he holds in his beak."

•

A happy bird of rapid growth
full of freshness and vigour with a wide wing span
that swerves from the flight path of the flock of other birds
and sets forth on its course alone.

Strange landscapes of a bursting memory
awaken beneath its feet, while it surveys
the area of mountains and crabs.

Its dilemma is made up of sand
from the sea and the sky; it does not know
whether to ascend or descend;
it only observes what it likes.

Then suddenly Famagusta emerges;
(they had described it correctly),
the bird feels its breast beating with wings.

In the beginning we spoke of "a broken spark" –
we retract that now; upright on its two feet,
full of a dazzling light
the spark kneels happily.

And she whispers in his ear "thousands of arrows,
fish and trees[165] are not enough to make
the city's beauty, even more precious.
We shall enter a museum, take great care.

---

164   the fish: a classical representation of a bird with a fish in its beak is found on a free-field style ancient vase at the Cyprus Museum.

165   thousands of arrows, fish and trees: elements of paintings on ancient free-field style ancient vases.

The horses and their ashes[166] in a corner
suffice to blow away your mind
and to fill you with dung."

•

The bird heeds caution and they enter through
a broken window – what joy
to see everything still there ... That's how it seemed to it.

Not even one of the free-field style vases were there
– alas! – to testify.
Empty were the glass display cases; a black hand
of the pillaged collection.

Hurriedly it turns its head. Long neck,[167]
crosses all around [swastikas][168] decorate
the utopia and long drawn out arches.[169]

Let's ascend the stairs, it whistles to the spark.

Following a silk ribbon they set off and go.

The bird's transparent song dries out
midway through hope – it hears the empty beat
of isolation – even its own grandfather
with the fish in his beak had left.

---

166 The horses and their ashes: the skeletons of two horses were found in one of the tombs of Salamis (8th/7th century BC). The skeletons were taken to the Municipality Museum of Famagusta.
167 Long neck: the birds on the ancient vases of free-field style have long necks. They are reminiscent of the migratory water birds that arrive every year at the Salt-Lake of Larnaca.
168 swastikas: swastikas are also found on the ancient vases of free-field style; they are an ancient symbol of life.
169 long drawn out arches: the Famagusta Museum building was a house of folkloric architecture with arches.

A mark was left where he had been
and a circle of dust.

"Let's get away from here," she says.
It wasn't speaking as a bird, it had turned into a woman
and fascinated, it followed her.

•

This transformation had to happen
so that the miracle could be revealed.
They come out into the light, it loses her from its sight
and it remains simply and solely a bird.

It was still cold and his heart stings
as it hears the sound of the dawn
inviting him for breakfast in the Garden.[170]

An agile gaze full of carnations.
Gymnasium (a Greek structure),
girls sailing through flowers,
the fish in the little lake, invigorated.

His mother had said: In the Timber Store[171]
(close to the cabarets and Savoy Hotel)
one day I fleetingly saw Spring.[172]
Truly, my child, in a two-wheeled cart,
pulled by two horses, and the charioteer
whose fat arms shone, was smiling,
certain that the prize was his.

---

170 the Garden: The Municipal Garden of Famagusta, at the entrance of the First Lyceum.
171 the Timber Store: a store owned by Mitsos Marangos who also built an important Library with books about Cyprus.
172 I saw Spring: c.1952. During the Festival, Spring was represented on a chariot pulled by horses.

Flowers, like sequins,
you'd think they were sewn with a needle,
were running to enter the Stadium of the Flower Festival.

(Barbed wire and sand bags, now.)

•

And since I am here, I should move on
said the Hyperborean bird[173] while gazing
at the embroidered banner of St Nicholas[174]
(they say it resembles Saint Sophia)
waving high in the sky;
formerly it was the distinguishing feature of the area –
with frigates in the bay and palm trees.

And a glance at St George the Exorcist[175]
who banishes every evil from the city.
It makes the sign of the cross standing in front of
simplistic icons – the castigation of Christ.

And at Saint Mary[176] of the Armenians
(one day his winged father in sailor shorts[177]
saw a crowd following a bride and groom strolling along in the light)
and the Frankish Church close to the house

---

173 the Hyperborean bird: The hyperborean maidens were companions of the God Apollo. Hyperborea was also the place of origin of the migratory birds that are depicted on the ancient vases of Salamis.

174 St Nicholas: The Cathedral of St Nicholas – a wonderful example of Gothic architecture – was begun by Lusignan and was completed in 1311 AD. During the siege of Famagusta by the Ottomans in 1571, the Cathedral was bombarded by the Ottoman artillery. It lost all its apses, except one. The Turks turned it into a mosque as they did the Cathedral of Saint Sophia in Nicosia. Experts believe that the Church of St Nicholas has the most elaborate designs (embroidered).

175 St George the Exorcist: Originally it was a church of the Nestorians, built in 1359 AD. According to popular belief the saint "exorcises" all evils.

176 Saint Mary: A chapel of an old Armenian monastery (14th century) close to the Martinengo Bastion, Famagusta Castle.

177 in sailor shorts: The poet must have been ten years old.

of the District Officer and the Jubilee Park,
near the Second High School (of Economics),
it knows it all, it wants to see it all.

Andonis Iliakis,[178] Theodosis Nicolaou,[179]
Georgios Fanos,[180] Skoteinos,[181] Comitis,[182]
Vasilakkas[183] ... The sun was also setting.
From the beach in front of the King George Hotel[184]
they spread their wings over the west,
flying to the leaves of the sky.

•

Its tears fall
here and there like pigeons from the head.
Oculus meus memoria est[185] – it says.

The Greeks are right when they say
they lack geographical knowledge – but not the birds.

The day begins to bring on the afternoon
to the hills and the valleys
with her plait on her shoulder
and singing from its ever-chirping mouth.

It saw itself in a mirror and said
to its image: "You are lying!"

---

178 Andonis Iliakis: Poet, accountant; migrated to London after the invasion.
179 Theodosis Nicolaou: Poet, Philologist, High School Principal in Larnaca after the invasion.
180 George Fanos: Poet and well-known doctor of Famagusta. Moved to Paphos after the invasion. An anti-conformist.
181 Skoteinos: a painter, now living in Agia Napa.
182 Comitis: an actor and now a TV producer in Nicosia.
183 Vasilakkas: a guitarist-singer. Died in London in 1977.
184 King George Hotel: sea-side hotel; the hangout of the poet's friends.
185 Oculus meus memoria est: a famous quote of St Bernard. "Oculus meus memoria est" (My eye is the memory).

By the stone wall it comes face to face with Andromache
tearing at her soul with her bare hands.

The Sun is the herald of darkness
– well studied in the firmament –
it turns night into a daring flare
as it strikes it in the eyes.

"Be gone light!" It commands.
The sun is dressed in black, like a groom,
night gives birth to a bridal dance,
the day is filled with wingless birds.

The tree looked at the sun thoughtfully
shaking its branches respectfully.
Its ears and eyes were teary,
– its foliage, I mean, with all its breasts.

The bird, full of fears and lures
fills its heart with sea and rocks.
Sometimes it stumbles on the banks of stony rivers
with subdued chirping
(knowing that a body
had been lying there for ever and it had deep roots)
sometimes its hope is like a horse full of sorrow.

"So, it was you then and no one else,
who committed this horrible act!"

He was speaking to his wife,
"The edges of your eyes are damp,
you must be looking for your ring in the lake."

Alarmed the bird resonates strangely
"… and you douse the whisper of the conversation."

Crickets with xylophones are heard;
tangled voices that you can't make out
to which bird they belong.

"My ring[186] fell in the lake of St Luke …"
Birds are knocking on the courtyard door
with their long beaks.
"Who is to enter and who is to leave?"
The bewildering song dries up.

On the denouement of the bird's song
the wine of the Universe is poured.
It could see the blood, the flesh
dressed nobly in the gardens.

The city, succumbing to sleepiness,
emerges bright and damp.

She was sleeping like Adam in the swaddling clothes of Paradise,
suddenly they took her rib and turned her into a Woman.

He sees the re-enactment of the scene
in a beloved city; but his children
have vanished, they have emigrated for good.
And he says "I have a glowing fire in my innards."

His eyelids are weighing him down, his neckline is trembling.

The rooster's dawn was getting its feeling back and the grinding stone
of time was bleached with a little of the sun's blood.

---
186 "my ring fell in the lake": cf. quote from the Greek folksong "The Bridge of Arta."

The waves, the sea's peel, stirred,
the eyes are simultaneously the image and its counterimage.
Pain contains the fermentation of life.[187]

The light of day – a purse made of hair[188]
love sealed with wax
the agonising cornerstone of the soul.[189]

Children of his who are returning;
but as the first leaf fell with the rain
they swallowed the little key of their voice.

The sun, like a full moon, looked at him.
The canopy of the tree sounded out its surroundings.
It sprang up joyfully. Glossolalia.
The gleaming voices of birds are shattered on rocks.
Birds' chirping that flared up in Gardens.
Rose-coloured mythical fish appear with swift fins!
The stars of the Heavens have been purified.

October 1980/October 1981

---

187 "Pain contains the fermentation of life": cf. quote from an interview of Jean-Louis Barrault, newspaper *To Vima*, 12 August 1980: "Pain is a bitter thing, but it contains the fermentation of life, the fermentation which allows us to capture the spiritual gift, a kind of acquired elation."
188 "purse made of hair" cf. *The Apocalypse of St John the Apostle*, v. 12–13.
189 the agonising cornerstone of the soul: op. cit. "These are some of my heroes who make up my internal family. The agonising heroes, full of passion, weak in the body but morally brave." Jean-Luis Barrault.

ABOUT THE AUTHOR AND THE TRANSLATOR

KYRIAKOS CHARALAMBIDES

Born in 1940 in Cyprus, he completed his primary and secondary education in Ammochostos (Famagusta) and then studied History and Archaeology at the University of Athens. He taught literature in secondary schools and he worked for thirty years at the Cyprus Broadcasting Corporation from where he retired as Director of Radio. He has published thirteen volumes of poetry, two volumes of essays and a translation of *Romanos the Melodist,* awarded the Hellenic Society of Literary Translators' Prize. Three of his books, amongst them *Ammochostos Vasilevousa* (*Famagusta Regina,* 1982), were awarded the Cyprus State Prize for Poetry; another book, *Tholos* (*Dome,* 1989), the Athens Academy Prize. His book *Methistoria* (*Meta-history,* 1995) was awarded the Hellenic Republic State Prize for Poetry. He has also received the International Cavafy Award (1998) as well as the Costas and Eleni Ouranis Prize from the Athens Academy for his entire poetic oeuvre (2003) and the Cyprus State Prize for Excellence in Literature (2007). He is a Doctor Honoris Causa of the Faculty of Letters, University of Athens (2013) and a Corresponding Member of the Academy of Athens (2013). Some of his books have been translated in eight languages.

JOHN MILIDES

Born in Zodhia, Cyprus and educated in Cyprus, Greece and Australia, he studied Greek and English literature at La Trobe University. He has taught Greek Language and Literature at Deakin University, La Trobe University, Monash University and Victoria University. He has published studies on Greek literature and he has translated Greek and Australian poetry. He has taught English poetry and poetry writing; a poetry anthology of his students' writing was published by Aquinas College in 2016. He now teaches at Marymede Catholic College. K. Charalambides' poetry collection *Tholos/Dome* was translated by J. Milides and published by La Trobe University in 2002.

www.ingramcontent.com/pod-product-compliance
Lightning Source LLC
Chambersburg PA
CBHW020937090426
42736CB00010B/1176